A keepsake of blessings and wisdom for new babies.

Letters to Baby

CHAZ CORZINE

BROADMAN
&HOLMAN
PUBLISHERS

Nashville, Tennessee

4262-99
0-8054-6299-6

Dewey Decimal Classification: 248.4
Subject Heading: CHRISTIAN LIFE / INFANTS
Library of Congress Card Catalog Number: 97-22693

Scriptures are quoted from the (KJV) King James Version; (NIV) the Holy Bible, New International Version, © 1973, 1978, 1984 by International Bible Society; (NKJV) New King James Version, © 1979, 1980, 1982, Thomas Nelson, Inc., Publishers; and (TLB) The Living Bible, © Tyndale House Publishers, Wheaton, Ill., 1971, used by permission.

Gloria Gaither's letter: © 1988 by Gloria Gaither. Originally published in We Have This Moment. Reprinted by Gaither Family Resources 1996. Used by permission.

Library of Congress Cataloging-in-Publication Data
Letters to baby / Chaz Corzine.
      p. cm.
   ISBN 0-8054-6299-6 (hardbound)
    1.Christian life. 2.Celebrities—United States—Religious life.
I. Corzine, Chaz, 1959– .
BV4529.L47   1997
305.232—dc21

                                        97-22693
                                          CIP

2 3 4 5 01 00 99 98 97

*This book is dedicated to
my wife, Deaver Mallory Corzine,
and our three beautiful children,
Sean, Mallory, and Allie.*

*Special thanks to Deaver
who was so instrumental in the dreaming,
working, and completion of this book.
I could not have done it without you,
nor would I have wanted to.*

LETTER CONTRIBUTORS

Ronald Reagan

Kathie Lee Gifford

Mario Andretti

Jack Kelley

Mark Victor Hansen

Jack Hanna

Kirk Cameron

Cal Thomas

Joe Garagiola

Michael and Debbie Smith

Edwin J. Staub

Mark Lowry

Franklin Graham

Dick Clark

Dave Dravecky

Alexander M. Haig Jr.

Max Lucado

Steve Allen

Frank Minirth

Bill Halamandaris

Sandi Patty

Tommy Lasorda

Michael S. Dukakis

Gary and Norma Smalley

Millard Fuller

Bill Bright

Ravi K. Zacharias

Joe White

James C. Dobson

Stephen Hicks

Tom and Alicia Landry

Robert H. Schuller

Faith Hill-McGraw and Tim McGraw

Patrick McCaskey

Mike Yaconelli

Amy Grant

Orel Hershiser

Robert A. Briner

Mary Fisher

Pat Robertson

Scott O'Grady

Wesley K. Stafford

Jim Bakker

Ara Parseghian

Rich Mullins

Art Linkletter

Greg Laurie

Michael Medved

Donny Osmond

Carman

Joe Gibbs

Charles Colson

Pat Boone

Wayne Watson

Frank E. Peretti

Luci Freed

Gloria Gaither

Bob Dole

Carl E. Hurley

Neil Lomax

Frank Schaeffer

Carol Everett

Liz Curtis Higgs

Brennan Manning

John Fischer

Howard G. Hendricks

Dan Quayle

INTRODUCTION

On June 11, 1991, my wife and I had our first child. He was 8 pounds 9 1/2 ounces, 21 1/2 inches long, and . . . he was perfect! We just stared at him in awe. I was amazed at the overwhelming love I felt for this beautiful baby. We had prayed for, planned for, and anticipated this moment for months—even years—but in an instant, I was a daddy . . . and would be forever!

I was so deeply affected by Sean's birth, I walked around in a daze—ecstatic beyond belief. I thought, literally, that God had hand-picked us to raise the most beautiful baby in the universe! I will never forget the first few moments of parenthood.

I have since learned that this is a universal feeling among first timers! But it's a great feeling, nonetheless!

Through my work with several great recording artists, I've been able to get to know many people I never dreamed I would even meet. One person I have had the privilege of meeting on several occasions is former President Ronald Reagan. Having always had a deep, abiding respect for this great man, I was greatly moved when he sent the following letter to my new son.

To be holding my precious son in my arms while reading such an inspiring letter, from someone whom I so greatly respected, filled me with encouragement and great hope for Sean's future. Like Sean, that letter is a precious gift.

Soon after receiving the president's letter, it occurred to me that it would be fun to see what words of encouragement or advice others might offer to newborn babies.

Each contributor to this book was asked the same question: "What would you tell a newborn baby that you have found to be important in life?"

Each letter is written from a perspective unique to the individual writer; consequently, a broad cross-section of our culture is represented. Many contributors are quite well known; others may be less familiar. And still others you may not know at all. But in each letter you will find a kernel of wisdom, the spark of inspiration for a life of promise and purpose.

Gratitude is deep for each person who participated in this project. As you will see, several of the writers have taken this opportunity to share very personal thoughts. This book enables you, as a new parent, to do the same. At the end of this book there is space waiting to be filled with your own "Letter to Baby." Then, at the proper time (sixteenth birthday, graduation from high school, etc.) you can share your hopes and dreams, written so many years before. It will be a cherished gift revealing the love that filled your heart . . . right from the beginning.

Dear Sean Louis,

Welcome! Your arrival today is a cause for joy far greater than you can know right now. In the years to come, you will fully understand how lucky you are to have been born in America to those who love you so deeply.

My hope is that you will realize the precious meaning of life in our nation and that you will always bear in your heart a special love for the freedoms we enjoy as a people. We live in a time when threats to human life and human freedom are at their zenith, and the world has dire need of people dedicated to their sacred cause. My prayer is that my generation and that of your parents will leave you a world made new in these values, so that you and your children's children can know that sublime joy which hovers by the cradle.

Take pride in whatever you do, keep faith with the blessings of your heritage, and remember the sacrifices so many have made before you to win the light of this day. Do these things, and you will return to this world a thousandfold the gift of your wonderful birth.

Mrs. Reagan and I join in sending you our best wishes for a long and fruitful life.

Ronald Reagan

KATHIE LEE GIFFORD

"Live with Regis and Kathie Lee" is one of the most popular shows of its type ever produced. Even with her incredibly busy schedule, Kathie Lee was one of the first people to respond when I started this book. Anyone who knows her or has seen her from afar knows of her love for children.

Dear Baby,

Welcome to the world. There's so much I would like to say to you, to warn you about, and to protect you from; but you have just arrived, and you'll have time for all of that as you get older.

So instead, I will share with you the one thing in your life I believe will be the most important truth you will ever hear. I hope that by learning it early and welcoming it into your young heart, it will be the most meaningful and invaluable source of joy and strength that you will ever need in your life's journey.

It is very simple, really—so simple that many people much older than you are stumble over it or struggle with it all of their lives. Yes, it is simple—simple but true.

Are you ready, little one? Whether you have been born into privilege or poverty; whether you have been born into suffering or health; and whether you have been born to two people who wanted you and planned you and welcomed you with joy—or you have been born to two people who didn't expect you, who for whatever reason have given you up, through their tears, to the care of others—nothing can change what I promise you is true:

God Loves You. You are precious, and He has a plan for your life.

So live your life, little one. Live it fully and fearlessly. Laugh often and cry when you must.

And know that you are His.

Love,

Kathie Lee

Kathie Lee

Mario Andretti

Mario Andretti is often referred to as the greatest race car driver of all time. In July 1993 he set the closed-course speed record at 234.275 mph. He is the first driver to win Indy car races in four decades and to win auto races in five decades. He continues to race, seeking the trophy at the twenty-four-hour LeMans.

Dear Baby,

Welcome to what I promise will be an exciting ride. Right now you are surrounded by people who love you, who care for you, and who are hoping you choose any profession other than mine!

Your parents have experienced great things in their lives, but none of their experiences can compare to the thrill they felt upon your arrival. In five decades of racing I had many great thrills, but none can compete with the day my own child was born. There is no greater gift than a child.

As you get older, you will grow to realize that your reputation is more important than anything you might accomplish; your friendships are more important than anything you acquire or win; and your word is more important than fame or success.

Grow to be a man or woman of your word, build strong friendships, and value people over any accomplishment. Do these things and you will make this world a better place.

I wish you the very best, little one.

Your friend,

Mario Andretti

Jack Kelley

Jack has one of the most unique per-
spectives from which to write. While
he has traveled all over the world,
interviewing literally every major head
of state for *USA Today*, his most recent
assignment has found him covering
war and tragedy throughout our world.
His compassion is evident in his
writing. He is one of the most widely
read newspaper journalists in the
world.

Dear Baby:

Preveyet! Do bro pozhalovat v mir!
(Hi! Welcome to the world!)

Greetings from Moscow! It's ice cold here, but your arrival has created a special warmth in the hearts of your loved ones. You're off to a great start! Hallelujah! Enjoy! Life is an adventure or it is nothing!

But be prepared: along the way, you'll be bombarded with images, messages, and philosophies all of which will be competing for your heart and mind. Stay strong. And pray for His wisdom.

Let me share with you two lessons He taught me on the world's battlefields. May they inspire you as they have me.

The first: give your life away. In Mogadishu, Somalia, during the 1993 civil war and famine, I watched as a bone-thin boy gave away his only food to his dying brother. The brother was so weak that the boy had to chew the piece of food for him, put it in his mouth, and then work his brother's jaw up and down to get him to swallow. The boy did this for weeks with nearly every piece of food he had.

Miraculously, the brother survived. But weeks later, the boy who fed him died of malnutrition. I guess that's what the Lord meant when He said there is no greater love than to lay down your life for someone else.

We may not be called to give our lives literally, but we must always remember to put others first.

Second: stand up for what you know is right, regardless of the cost. In Kuwait City after the 1991 Gulf War, I spoke with a Kuwaiti teenager who had been beaten beyond belief by Iraqi soldiers. Each night, he would sneak out of his home to deliver food to elderly Kuwaitis in the neighborhood who were afraid to leave their homes.

The Iraqis demanded to be told where the elderly Kuwaitis lived so they could rob and beat them too. But the teenager refused to give in and, after two days of beatings, was left for dead by the retreating Iraqis.

I remember thinking, *If he can stand up for his family, friends, and country, then I can do the same for my God.*

These two people, the Somali brother and the Kuwaiti teenager, are my heroes. There's got to be a special place in heaven for people like them.

I believe you, too, can have a heart of gold. You were born at this time for a reason. Go for it. Never look back.

And always remember: Be naive enough to think that you can change the world—and you will.

I'll be praying for your generation every step of the way!

Jack Kelley,
Foreign Correspondent

Mark Victor Hansen

For more than twenty years Mark Victor Hansen has focused on the vital elements of human behavior that most affect the outcome of personal and professional lives. Mark is in high demand as a keynote speaker and seminar leader by many of North America's top corporations and professional associations. He is known as "The Master Motivator." During his career of more than two decades, his message has reached more than one million people—live—in virtually every major city in the United States and Canada.

In addition to his motivational speaking, Mark is also a prolific writer, with many best-selling books. *Chicken Soup for the Soul*, with its universal themes ranging from love and positive attitudes to humor and relationships, has been awarded "1994 Book of the Year" by more than twenty thousand bookstores nationwide.

MARK VICTOR HANSEN
*"Motivation for the
Betterment of Humanity."*

Dear Baby,

My soul rejoices with your entrance into this human experience, into the world we now share. You are God's greatest miracle: a living, breathing, feeling, handiwork of the Most High.

I wish for you that you will be loved, guided, nurtured, inspired, excited, and challenged by those who have the responsibility to raise you to adulthood. I hope that you will recognize your unique talents and live to realize your fullest potential.

I want you to always know that you have the ultimate power in your grasp—the power to make a choice. You may not be able to choose success or failure, poverty or riches, good health or illness, but you can always choose your own reaction to your experiences. Whatever the world may give you, you can respond with love, compassion, caring, and a desire to serve your fellow man. It is your choice to employ your innate genius to make an extraordinary difference—to serve greatly with passion.

You do not belong to yourself; we all belong to life. Know that you are a thread in the woven fabric of life, and without you the weaving will not be complete. You are an integral and important part of God's great plan. Take great care of the body you have been given; it is the only one you will receive. Treat yourself with tenderness, and do nothing to harm it.

The most important thing I want to share with you is to always remember that you own a divine connection with God inside of your soul. You are never alone or rejected—if you ever feel this way it is because you have turned your back on this connection. Find a quiet place, away from the busy trappings of our world, and renew your connection—it will always be there for you. When you feel connected with God, your life will be filled with delight, laughter, love, joy, and a passion for all that life holds in store.

Love and blessings,

Mark Victor Hansen

Jack Hanna

Most people like animals, but few like animals as much as Jack Hanna does! He has become America's favorite animal expert. Jack is both entertaining and respected. He is Director Emeritus for the Columbus Zoo and with his many TV appearances, he is considered a spokesman for all zoos. I love how Jack's letter reflects his specific perspective.

Columbus Zoo

Dear Baby,

Welcome—you've just opened your eyes on an amazing world!

Of all the fantastic things that you may experience in your time here on planet Earth, I dare say that you will fall in love with animals.

You can learn some interesting things by watching them! You'll see that lions live in family groups and that any one of the mother lions will take care of any of the cubs—even if the cub is not hers!

Monkeys live in groups so that all the baby monkeys are well cared for; thus, the babies have the advantage of learning about life from their moms and dads, brothers and sisters, aunts and uncles, and a variety of other family members.

One thing they all share in common is that they have to coexist in nature in perfect harmony—a delicate balance inspired by God. So take care of the world; it's their home too.

Life is precious and somewhat open-ended—what you put into it is often what you will get back in return. With that in mind, have a zest for whatever you pursue, and be enthusiastic about your beliefs!

All the best,

Jack Hanna

Jack Hanna

Kirk Cameron

Kirk is a fine actor who has consistently stood for his beliefs in a business and a city where that is not always popular. He has had great success in series TV as well as feature film. Of all his accomplishments, however, Kirk would tell you he is most proud of his marriage to Chelsea Noble and his role as a new daddy.

Dear Baby,

Welcome to life! So many people have been waiting for you to get here and are so excited! How you got here is pretty exciting too—you'll have to ask your parents about that when you get older.

All babies come from God but He sends them to their parents in different ways. Some babies are made in their mommies' tummy, and some are made in someone else's tummy and then sent "special delivery" to your mommy and daddy. Pretty exciting, huh? Either way, you can be sure that you are a very special gift from God, and your parents love you very much.

There is lots to learn about being a kid. Sometimes it's tough, so here are a few tips that will help you get a good head start in life:

1. Learn how much Jesus loves you and then love Him back with all your heart.
2. Don't ever think of yourself as more important or better than someone else.
3. Do special things for your family and friends to show them how much you love them.

Do these three things and you'll be ready for a very exciting life. Hang on, it's an adventurous ride.

Just in case one day you decide you're not as old as you'd like to be, don't worry; you will be soon. Maybe not as soon as you'd like, but God has a very special reason for that. (You'll find the answer to that one when you're a lot older.) Remember, kids have lots of special privileges older people don't. And do you want to know a grown-up secret? A lot of grown-ups wish they could be your age instead! It's true!

I have one place to recommend for you to go for fun. It's called "nature." It's the most fun playground there is, and it's humongous! I like the ocean part and the stream part the best, but there are lots more parts that are really cool too—like the mountain part where you can see the world shrunk down to miniature size below or the forest part where all the big trees live. Ask your mom and dad to take you there; you'll like it!

Your life is going to be so much fun! There will also be times when you will be sad or maybe a little scared. But there's good news! You can always pray and tell God what you need, and He will take care of things for you. You see, He is always watching over you and is with you wherever you go. Just look for Him and you'll know what I mean.

Well, have fun, and remember: you have made so many people happy just by being yourself. Keep it up, and always know how special you are.

Kirk Cameron

CAL THOMAS

Americans know Cal Thomas through his regular appearances in print (his syndicated column appears twice a week in more than four hundred newspapers) and from his many TV appearances. He hosted his own show on CNBC. Among Thomas's most striking features are his boldness and honesty. The author of nine books, he has journeyed through the American educational establishment, identifying what he believes is wrong with it and what must be done to change it. He is straightforward about his stance on many cultural issues, with particular attention paid to taxpayer-funded, public education—one of the most divisive issues facing Americans today.

Los Angeles Times
SYNDICATE

Cal Thomas

Dear Baby,

"There is nothing new under the sun," wise King Solomon once said. Everything that you think will have been thought before. Everything you try will have been tried by someone else, long before you were born.

The secret to a successful life is learning from those older than you so that you won't have to repeat their mistakes (you'll still have time for making plenty of your own!).

Because there is no one "older" than God, seek first His wisdom and His kingdom, and everything else will be given to you as you need it. Because God loves you, even more than your parents, and sees the future and knows what is best for you, you can always rely on Him to do what is best for you.

You are fortunate to have been born into a family that loves you and loves God. Honor them, by honoring Him; and honor Him, by honoring them (it is the first commandment with a promise).

May the Lord Jesus become part of your early life and remain at the center of your life for as long as He gives you breath, and then forever.

God bless and keep you.

Cal Thomas

JOE GARAGIOLA

Joseph Henry Garagiola grew up on Elizabeth Street in the St. Louis neighborhood called "The Hill." He was signed to his first baseball contract at age sixteen. Garagiola played for the Cardinals in for five seasons, including the 1946 championship year. After his pro career ended in 1954, he joined St. Louis radio station KMOX and broadcast Cardinals games the next year. After moving to the Yankees, Garagiola called baseball for NBC for twenty- seven years. Two stints with "The Today Show" capped his illustrious broadcast career. A 1973 winner of television's Peabody Award, Joe Garagiola entered the broadcaster's wing of the Baseball Hall of Fame in 1991.

Joe Garagiola
Paradise Valley, Arizona 85253

Dear Baby,

Welcome! Your being here tells us all that God has plans for you. It's up to you to realize this and recognize God's intentions. In all you do, try to look beyond yourself. You'll be amazed at what you can accomplish. As the great Jackie Robinson, who accomplished so much, always said, "A life is not important except in the impact it has on other lives."

I've been around sports my whole life so I've learned many of my lessons there. In sports you don't talk about it—you do it. Don't tell me you can hit; go out and hit. Sports gives everybody a chance and asks only "Can you do it?" Just go out and show you can. Don't look at the other guy. The only one you have to please is in the mirror.

Remember to dream big dreams. Life will make you laugh and make you cry. Don't be afraid to do either one. When you are in doubt, treat others the way you want to be treated. Then the road has fewer potholes. When it's decision time, I rely on the following prayer and it works every time: God grant me serenity to accept the things I cannot change, . . . courage to change the things I can, . . . and the wisdom to know the difference.

Now enjoy the ride. It will be exciting.

Sincerely,

Joe Garagiola

Joe Garagiola

Michael W. Smith

"Smitty," as he is known to friends, drove his parents' car to Nashville in 1978 in hopes of being able to publish his music. He had no idea, at that time, that he would not only record his own music, but that his music would go on to sell more than seven million copies. He has achieved tremendous success in both the contemporary Christian field and the mainstream music market. More important, however, is that Michael and Debbie Smith are the parents of five beautiful children.

Michael and Debbie wrote one of Michael's greatest hits, "Friends."

Dear Baby,

Welcome to this world where you were called into being for just this time, this place! Do you know that your maker, God, your heavenly Father, knit you together? That before you were created so miraculously in your mother's womb, God saw your unformed body? And that He has already recorded every day of your life in His massive heavenly diary even before the day of your birth? Can you believe He even knows the first word you'll say and every one after that before you say it?

How we wish we could welcome you to a sin-free, constantly happy, wondrously-loving world where you will always be cherished and appreciated for your uniqueness. We regret that we cannot, since the very first man and woman rejected God's instructions in just such a perfect world. We're afraid that you, and every other baby ever born, are born into sin, that terrible turning away from God. It only leads to heartache and loneliness because sin separates us from the very reason we were created—to love and fellowship with our Creator!

But we have great news for you, little one! God sent His own Son as a precious baby (just like you) to this earth. He grew and lived and loved and then died to make a way for you to know that incredible sin-free, happy, loving relationship with God. So our prayer and greatest hope for you is that you get to know Jesus (God's Son) and that you believe He is your Savior from all the death in this life. Then you will truly love, and the limits of your life will be determined by only God Himself!

So blessings as you sleep and eat and grow and learn . . . and may Jesus be the light of your life.

Love,
Michael and Debbie

EDDIE STAUB

The executive director of the Eagle Ranch is Eddie Staub. Eagle Ranch provides a Christ-centered home for boys ages six to eighteen who are in need of a stronger family support system. The goal at the ranch is the spiritual, intellectual, emotional, social, and physical development of the children and the hopeful reunification with the children's natural families.

EAGLE **ER** RANCH

Dear Son or Daughter,

Our world is crying out for godly leaders—men and women who dare to be different as they follow God's plan for their lives.

I want to share three important truths about godly leaders: their willingness to stand alone, to serve others, and to choose friends wisely.

Standing alone means yielding to the Holy Spirit's pressure from within to do what is right, rather than giving in to the pressure from without to compromise your convictions.

A true servant is one who serves simply because there's a need; he's not driven by a desire for recognition. The essence of servanthood is a willingness to be inconvenienced.

Finally, a godly leader is careful about the friends he chooses. As Proverbs 13:20 says, "He who walks with the wise grows wise, but a companion of fools suffers harm" (NIV). Please understand, you will reflect those with whom you associate; you will mirror their values, morals, and the depth and breadth of their goals.

In living out your high calling to be God's kind of leader, rely on His Holy Spirit to empower and equip you day by day.

God's blessings and peace.

Sincerely,

Edwin J. Staub

Mark Lowry

Mark Lowry has been delivering hilari-
ous comedy to crowds for years—on
the road, in his popular recordings,
and on his award-winning videos. His
Bible Belt humor and stories of growing up in the church have brought him
laughter and fans wherever he travels.
Mark's letter is a glimpse into this
incredibly creative character.

MARK LOWRY PRODUCTIONS

Hey kid! Wake up! What are you gonna do, sleep your life away? Ah, go ahead and sleep. You'll have the rest of your life to be awake.

Welcome to the wonderful world of awe!

You have started a fascinating journey, and there's one thing I want to tell you—don't miss it! Right now you're in awe of everything. Don't ever lose that. Stay in awe. It's a wonderful place to live. Go on and stare for hours at a light. Basically you'll spend your first few months staring, crying, and messing your britches. To some adults it seems like such a waste of time. But I agree with you, lights are interesting and messing your britches can be warm and comforting (at first)!

You are rich. We all are. If we can eat anytime we want, we're rich. Life is short. It really will be over before you know it. So live while you're here, 'cause you're gonna be dead a long time.

Looks are not important. Oh they are when you're a teenager. But when you go to your twentieth high school reunion, you'll see that looks don't last.

Your mom and dad love you a lot, so when you become a teenager, go easy on 'em. This is the first time they've ever been parents. One day you'll be a parent. Your parents will be grandparents. They'll have parenting down by then, and they'll be happy to share it with you. And then when you do become a parent go easy on your kids—because one day they'll decide what nursing home you go to.

God's mercies are new every morning because you'll wear them out every day.

Always remember: "i" before "e" except after "c."

When you're out of money you can't just write a check.

Turn the lights out when you leave a room.

Become potty trained as soon as possible. You don't know it now, but you're really making a mess.

Everything you see was created by a word from God. Except one thing—you. When you look at the stars, you're looking at something that was created by a word from God. When you look at the mountains, you're looking at something that was created by a word from God. But when you look in the mirror, always remember: you're looking at something that was created by the very hand of God.

Still in awe,

Mark Lowry

Franklin Graham

Franklin Graham is the son of Billy and Ruth Graham. Through his organization, Samaritan's Purse, Franklin delivers medical supplies to areas in need all over the world. His Operation Christmas Child program delivers shoeboxes filled with toys to nearly two million needy children throughout the world.

Dear Baby,

As you come into this world, some may say, "Good luck." However, luck has nothing to do with getting you through this life.

The world in which you have arrived is filled with social problems, political instability, and economic failure. Catastrophic environmental problems await you and your generation. There are food shortages and diseases that modern science may never solve.

You now live in an ever changing world. There will be times when there seems to be no hope. You have been born with something that every human being since the first man, Adam, has been afflicted with—the universal disease called sin. Sin is disobedience to God—breaking His law. The Bible says that we have all sinned and come short of God's glory and that the wages of sin is death, but the gift of God is eternal life through Jesus Christ our Lord.

God in heaven made you and wants to guide and direct your every step. He loves and cares for you. You will be constantly faced with temptation. God has given you a free will to exercise as you choose. You will make many decisions as you walk through life. Your heavenly Father has a special purpose and plan for your life, and He wants to reveal it to you. God, in His great love, has provided a way to cure the problem of sin. The Bible, God's holy Word, tells us in John 3:16: "For God so loved the world that he gave his only begotten Son, that whosoever believeth in Him should not perish, but have everlasting life" (KJV).

God's only Son, Jesus Christ, took your sin and died in your place. He gave His life as a ransom for you. One day soon, you will be faced with a decision to accept or reject Him. God will forgive and cleanse you if you repent of your sin and place your faith and trust in His Son. This world is a dark place, filled with sorrow and despair; but Christ and Christ alone gives us hope and light in this sin-sick world. If you let Him, He will give you meaning and purpose to life and satisfy your every longing. Put your faith and trust in Jesus Christ, and accept Him as your Lord and Savior. He will never leave you or fail you.

May God richly bless you, and may you live to glorify our Savior in heaven.

Sincerely,

Franklin Graham

Dick Clark

"America's oldest living teenager," Dick Clark is one of the most recognized and popular personalities in American entertainment history. His show, "American Bandstand," provided the musical backdrop to the lives of a generation of Americans. He has been inducted into the Rock and Roll Hall of Fame and the Academy of Television Arts and Sciences Hall of Fame.

Dear Baby,

You're about to start on a very interesting journey. It's called life.

Life is full of twists and turns. Many of the things that happen to you will be unpredictable. Try as best you can to plan your journey. If you can figure out where you're headed early on, and put some direction into the journey, you'll get the fullest enjoyment out of it.

You'll be making some side trips, but don't get discouraged. The most important word of advice anyone can give you is: "Don't give up." Determination will help you through life's journey. Please have a wonderful experience.

Sincerely,

Dick Clark

DAVE DRAVECKY

Dave Dravecky was a pitcher in the
major leagues for eight years. A malig-
nant tumor in his pitching arm eventually required amputation of his arm
and shoulder to save his life. Today he
and his wife Jan encourage people who
struggle with life-and-death situations
through their organization called Dave
Dravecky's Outreach of Hope.

Dear Baby,

You're finally here. We have all been waiting with excitement for this very special day—your birthday!! As I gaze into your eyes, I am just amazed at how beautiful you are. And to think that you are our baby. But then I stop and think, Are you really mine? Yes and no. You are God's child, and He has entrusted your life to your mom and me. I must confess that I am scared. I've never done this before. Your mom and I are as new to this as you are new to entering this world. Please know that our desire is to give you our best, and yet we know that there will be times when we mess up. When we do, Baby, please forgive us. I'm sure there will be plenty of times when we must forgive you. But please know that our love for you is unconditional.

There is so much we want to do for you and tell you about, but for now and the next several years, we want you to enjoy life to the fullest, and we promise we will do all we can to make that possible.

As you begin this journey of life, you will be exposed to so much. Both good and bad will come knocking at your door. The challenge for your mom and me will be to give you all the tools you will need to make the right choices. These tools have been given to us by God, and we are now beginning the process of passing them on to you.

I know I've rattled on and it's getting close to naptime, but being eager to get you started in the "school of life," I'd like to leave you with two passages from God's Word. (By the way, you should have this book, the Bible, read by the time you're in first grade. Just kidding!)

My prayer for you is that you will grow to "trust in the Lord with all your heart and lean not on your own understanding; in all your ways acknowledge him, and he will make your paths straight" (Prov. 3:5–6, NIV) and that you will dwell on "whatever is true, whatever is noble, whatever is right, whatever is pure, whatever is lovely, whatever is admirable . . . excellent or praiseworthy" (Phil. 4:8, NIV).

For now, as you begin your nap, sleep well. Our journey will last a lifetime together. More than anything, I hope we will become the best of friends and that Jesus will become your best friend.

I love you!

Your dad,

Dave Dravecky

Alexander M. Haig Jr.

As a soldier, statesman, and respected advisor to six presidents of the United States, Alexander Meigs Haig Jr. has rendered a lifetime of extraordinary service to his country and to the international community of freedom-loving nations.

The full measure of General Haig's contribution to the nation is apparent in his continuing service to his fellow citizens. He has served on three presidential commissions. He has unstintedly participated in the education of our nation's future leaders, lecturing extensively at colleges and universities. He is a published author of the foreign affairs and diplomatic history of the Cold War era.

Dear Baby,

What a wonderful world you have entered, and what joy you have brought to your parents and family. But rejoicing is not the only sentiment your arrival has inspired. Indeed, I find myself guilty of envy as I consider the opportunities you will find awaiting you in the century ahead.

Modern technology in, among other things, information sciences, medicine, and transportation have transformed the globe and created heretofore unimaginable opportunities. You will be able to participate successfully in this wondrous new age to the degree that you hold firmly to the principles that have themselves been central to the generation of the achievements you have inherited. Foremost among these principles are love of God, country, and family.

Welcome aboard!

Alexander M. Haig Jr.

MAX LUCADO

This pastor from Oak Hills Church of Christ in San Antonio, Texas, is known throughout the world as one of the most important writers in the Christian market. Max's titles include *No Wonder They Call Him Savior*, *Six Hours One Friday*, and *When God Whispers Your Name*. His recent *In the Grip of Grace* is one of my favorites.

MAX LUCADO

Dear Baby,

Ever since your arrival today, the world has been shouting. Shouting with joy. Shouting with pride. Shouting with hope.

But tonight the shouting ceased, and I heard a whisper. I placed my finger in your tiny hand, and your fingers wrapped around mine. Purely by instinct, you squeezed the hand of your father.

Life whispered to me, "This is a holy moment."

In the years ahead, my sweet child, your hand will hold hundreds of others. Your hand will embrace your mother's as you struggle to take your first steps. Your hand will be in mine as I show you how to hold a pencil. A hand larger than yours will lead you up the stairs to your first day of school.

I'll hold your hand as we walk to church, explore the neighborhood, and take long walks.

And someday, all too soon, your hand will know the brush of romance. In front of candles and friends, someone will hold your hand and slide a ring on your finger. In time, you'll likely feel what I felt tonight—the magical squeeze of your own child's hand around your finger.

Life whispers in such moments. And in that moment tonight I whispered as well. I whispered a prayer. I prayed you'd spend the rest of your life doing what you did tonight. May you ever hold the hand of your Father, your heavenly Father.

Love,

Daddy

STEVE ALLEN

Steve Allen is a legendary performer and widely respected as one of the great minds in the entertainment world. He created and was the first host of "The Tonight Show." Steve has also recorded forty albums, and written more than four thousand songs and nearly fifty books. He is, of course, a member of the Television Academy Hall of Fame.

STEVE ALLEN

Dear Baby,

You are a fortunate child, indeed. You have a mother and father who are not only committed to each other and to you, but also to the important values that they obviously hope will in time be perceived as important as they, in fact, are.

With such parents I'm sure you will discover, earlier than most children, the importance of reading. For unknown ages there was literally no such thing as the human ability to read. Humans were able to communicate, of course, but the process by which they gradually figured out a method for converting their sighs, smiles, shouts, moans, and murmurings into visible symbols represents one of the greatest human achievements.

Like many of mankind's accomplishments it is scarcely appreciated at all today, so I would urge you to keep the freshness of outlook that most children have but most adults have lost.

Secondly, I suggest that you appreciate your individual good fortune because already you have a tremendous advantage over billions of other children and adults around the world.

One of the discoveries that almost everyone in time makes is that there is no natural fairness to life, no natural justice in the universe. What little justice we actually encounter is all imposed by particular humans, and we certainly need larger armies of good people doing such admirable work.

Eventually, when you are older, you will encounter the ongoing debate of how best to increase fairness and diminish injustice for those who live in poverty and ignorance. In fact, I think you could do nothing more praiseworthy with your own life than devote it to the cause of human brotherhood and social justice.

It was out of the crying need for justice that humankind developed the means by which freedom was increased. Freedom and democracy, you see, are not part of the natural order of social events. Tyranny, dictatorship and harshness have been the norm throughout history and prehistory. The American freedoms that are guaranteed by our Constitution were developed very late in the large process of human development, and even now there are those who think the establishment of them was a mistake.

I follow the progress of your generation with great interest—at least to the extent my few remaining years permit—and I have little doubt that you will do well because of the support you are currently receiving.

One last thought. Not even the world's wisest philosophers have ever explained how we have been so fortunate as to have developed a sense of humor, but we do know that it is not simply a trivial and playful thing. It is, rather, fundamental to human happiness. Consequently, you should feel free to have as much sheer, simple fun as you now do in the innocence of your early childhood. But determine never to lose that sweet, playful approach to life. You will enjoy living better if you retain the ability to smile and laugh, and others will be attracted to you because of your ability to recognize what is laughable and even sometimes absurd about the human condition.

With love and warmest good wishes,

Steve Allen

Frank Minirth

Dr. Frank Minirth is the director of the
Minirth Clinic in Richardson, Texas. He
also hosts a live call-in radio program
dealing with a variety of medical,
emotional, and spiritual issues. He has
authored or co-authored more than
forty books on the subjects of emotional
and relational wholeness.

Dear Baby,

You are one in a thousand—one chance in a thousand to even be born today, one chance in a thousand to be born in America, one chance in a thousand to be born to Christian parents, one chance in a thousand to be born in an environment where you can learn to communicate well with others, one chance in a thousand to be mentally healthy, once chance in a thousand to hear sweet Christian music, one chance in a thousand to hear God's dear Word read daily, one chance in a thousand to hear of our wonderful Jesus Christ, one chance in a thousand to walk with Him, one chance in a thousand to share Him with others, one chance in a thousand in innumerable ways.

You are one in a thousand!

In Christ,

Frank Minirth, M.D

Frank Minirth, M.D.

The Minirth Clinic || *A Matter Of Caring*

Bill Halamandaris

Bill Halamandaris is cofounder and president of The Caring Institute, which was established in Washington D.C., in 1985 to teach the value of caring. The National Caring Awards were established to identify particularly caring Americans. The institute also operates the Frederick Douglas Museum and Hall of Fame for Caring Americans.

CARING
INSTITUTE

Dear Baby,

As you enter this world, please know how precious you are. In you, the entire human race is again reborn. You are all there is, all there ever was, all that will be.

You are Atlas. You carry the world on your tiny shoulders. The seed of the past, you are the promise of the future. You are God's opinion that the world should go on.

As you open your eyes, you will notice a lot of grown-ups around you acting strange. They will laugh and smile a lot. They will want to touch you, hug you, hold you, and kiss you. They will make funny faces and forget themselves in your presence—if only for a moment—and be at their best.

As you grow older, the impact you have on other people will not always be as obvious, and what you bring out in them may not always be their best. But live with the knowledge that you will always have that power—the power to touch and move, love and inspire, comfort and console. You also have the power to hurt and humiliate, defeat and destroy. So choose wisely, my young friend.

Know that you will change the world with everything you do or do not do—this is your birthright and your responsibility. Try to be the light.

You will be blessed to the same degree and in equal measure to the blessings God confers on others through you.

With love and best wishes,

Bill Halamandaris

SANDI PATTY

Sandi Patty is one of the most gracious
and kind people I know. Any given
week in her year might include an
appearance for the president or a soft-
ball game with one of her children. She
would handle either with grace and
charm. Sandi is another contributor
who chose this book as an outlet for a
very personal letter. This letter is to
her newly adopted child.

Sandi Patty

Dearest Baby,

I don't even know where to begin. The unexpected delight of welcoming you into our home has been such cause for giggles and tears these past two days. We can't wait to go to the hospital and pick you up tomorrow and bring you home!! Yes, that's right—home!!! Your new house with your new family. What a gift you already are to us.

I know you'll like your home and family. We're kinda wild but we have so much love to share, and we can't wait to share it with you. We have so much we want to tell you, so much we want to give you, and so much we want you to learn. But I guess we don't have to teach you everything on the first day. We've got plenty of time.

We live in a world that is always changing. We live in a country that is always growing. We live in a city and state that is constantly being shaped by the times and needs of its people. It can be a pretty scary place. And it may seem like with all the changing and growing that there isn't much you can count on. Even our family goes through changes and seasons as each of us continues to grow in this process of "becoming."

I don't say all of this to discourage you during your first days of life. I simply point all of this out to you so that this profound promise that I really want to share with you will make an impact. It's not really eloquent, and yet it's the most beautiful thing that I've ever heard. It's not really theologically profound, and yet it is the very anchor on which our faith is built. It's best said in the words of this song that we will teach you and will sing with you for years to come:

Yes, Jesus loves me.

Yes, Jesus loves me.

Yes, Jesus loves me.

The Bible tells me so.

Through all the joys and disappointments you may face in your little life, you can always count on that promise. It's true—I know it is.

So, little one, welcome to the world. Welcome to the big white house, with the big back yard, with lots and lots of kids, and lots and lots of love.

With much, much love from your loving and grateful mom.

Tommy Lasorda

Tommy Lasorda is known as the "dean" of major league managers. As the manager of the Los Angeles Dodgers, he guided his team to two World Series championships and four National League pennants. Tommy Lasorda is one of the world's most recognized and beloved sports figures.

LOS ANGELES Dodgers®

Dear Baby,

I am very happy to welcome a future Dodger into the world!

Every step you take in life leads you along the path to a bright future, and you will be supported and surrounded by family and friends who love you very much. As you mature you will come to appreciate this great country of America as much as I do. My mother and father came to America from Italy and settled in Norristown, Pennsylvania. It was there they provided much love for me and my four brothers. I know your parents will care for you, make sacrifices for you, and teach you to respect others and yourself, just as my wonderful parents did for me. These are two of the greatest gifts we can give to others and ourselves: love and respect—for God, family, and America.

Take pride in whatever course you choose in life. Work hard, set your goals high, and you will surely go far in life.

Sincerely,

Tommy Lasorda
Tommy Lasorda

MICHAEL DUKAKIS

Michael Dukakis, the son of Greek immigrants, has held numerous elected positions and was elected governor of Massachusetts three times. In 1996 his colleagues in the National Governor's Association voted him the most effective governor in the nation. He won the Democratic nomination for the presidency in 1988.

Dear Baby,

Flowers are everywhere, and it's about seventy degrees—more than enough reason to inspire optimism about the future and especially about your future.

You and your friends will be living in a world that is more peaceful than any we have ever lived in. The Cold War is over! At the same time it is a world in which we are still searching for the kind of society and sense of community that is life at its very best. And the United States is the one best hope for demonstrating what that kind of society and that sense of community really mean.

But it won't happen unless you and many young people growing up in a new century get deeply and actively involved in the politics and public life of their times. It won't be easy. There will be difficult and frustrating moments along the way. We can tell you, however, from our own experience, that there is nothing more fulfilling or satisfying in life than being of service to others.

Happy landing! Enjoy the love of your parents and your family.

Study hard and take advantage of the wonderful educational opportunities that this country gives you. Get involved in your community, state, and country, and you will never regret it.

Sincerely,

Michael S. Dukakis

Gary Smalley

Gary Smalley is one of the country's foremost experts on relationships. He is the author of twelve best-selling books and the host of several films and videos on the subject. His "Love Is a Decision" seminars have attracted more than 200,000 people and literally millions have seen Gary's infomercials featuring his video series, "Hidden Keys to Loving Relationships." Gary and his wife, Norma, have used this opportunity to write a letter to their new grandbabies.

Dear Grandbabies,

What an exciting time to have you join us. We have thanked the Lord for you many times and asked Him to give us the grace to love you the way that pleases Him the most. You've come at a time when Grandpa and Grandma are thrilled to pass along to you what we believe are two of the greatest ways to live and enjoy life to the fullest. We're not only planning to be your example, but we will look for every opportunity to reinforce those principles in your life. We can hardly wait to see how the Lord will enrich your life and create a godly light in this darkened world.

First we want to show you how important it is to honor everything God has created. When you're old enough, you'll understand the picture Grandma has put on your wall. It tells all about how beautiful God has made everything. We hope you'll agree with us that the Lord is good and everything about Him reflects love and value. He even wants us to "fix our thoughts only on things that are true and honorable, lovely, pure and admirable . . . things that are excellent and worthy of praise." That's what He tells us in Philippians 4:8. Your Grandma and I try to see His beauty in everything. We realize that He wants us to place the highest value on Him and then continue valuing each and every precious thing He has created. We respect the trees and water, the beautiful mountains and prairies, and all of His people no matter what race or culture they're from. If we can see it, we treasure it as given to us from Him. We try not to use words that degrade or hurt any part of His creation. Sometimes we mess up, and when we do, we try to make it right again by seeking forgiveness or by repairing what we have damaged. We're always mindful that God's creation is worth taking our time to care for.

The second greatest principle that guides our life, and hopefully yours someday, is to keep our anger as low as possible every day. We don't want the sun to go down on any emotions that make up anger: mainly our frustrations, our fears, and our hurts. You'll find that unloading these emotions every day will keep you alive with the Lord and with the ability to honor Him. When we allow anger to creep into our hearts and stay there, we close out the Lord and the ability to keep on loving others like He wants us to. Someday you'll read this in 1 John 2:9–11. You'll also repeat someday what has become known as the Lord's Prayer. Part of the Lord's Prayer is about forgiving others so that God can forgive you. Jesus taught us that the reason God can't forgive us if we don't forgive others is that He can't reach us when we're unforgiving. When anger fills our hearts, we're in darkness, and He only lives in the light.

If you keep these two powerful truths at the tip of your heart, you'll find life much more enjoyable and full. God gives wisdom to those who learn to honor Him and to those who learn to find value even in the things that hurt us. Always remember that He can turn sorrow into joy, ashes into beauty, and through any trial you'll ever face, He can use the trial to make you an "oak of righteousness." We'll pray for you every day and ask the Lord to bless you beyond measure.

We love you!

Grandpa & Grandma

Grandpa and Grandma (Gary and Norma Smalley)

Millard Fuller

Millard Fuller, an attorney and businessman, had an idea to make shelter a "matter of conscience," so that one day everyone would have at least a simple, decent place to live. Thus, he founded Habitat for Humanity in 1976. By 1992 there were more than eight hundred affiliates of Habitat across the United States and active projects in forty foreign countries.

Dear Baby!

Voilà! Here you are. You got your start about nine months ago, but the world you're now in is a whole lot older.

Who are you? What will you become? What contributions or problems will you add to the world during your life on earth?

All of these questions have no answer as you slowly develop among the others of us who arrived ahead of you.

I know nothing of your family. I don't even know your color or your sex. I don't know your neighborhood or the religious and political beliefs of your family. I don't know whether or not you come from a fully functional family or even if your parents love each other.

I do know this: God loves you. Your birth was not some meaningless accident of nature. There is a purpose for your existence and that purpose was set in your genes and in every fiber of your being as you were being formed in your mother's womb.

Will you fulfill your God ordained purpose? That's up to you because God has given the greatest gift of all: a free will. You get to decide.

You will learn about Jesus at some point in your life. Your parents may teach you about this Man who was born two thousand years ago. If they don't teach you about Jesus, you will hear about Him from someone else. What you believe about Jesus is your choice. I do urge you to seriously consider Jesus. Just never forget: God loves you.

You may live on earth for only a very short time, or you may live for many years. In either case, God will always love you. People along life's way may disappoint you, hurt you, or be unkind to you. But God's love is always there for you. Isn't that wonderful? Never forget it. That assurance will help you time and time again in the years ahead.

In God's love,

Millard Fuller

BILL BRIGHT

Bill Bright is the founder and president of Campus Crusade for Christ International, an interdenominational ministry committed to taking the gospel of Jesus Christ to all nations. The ministry cooperates with millions of Christians from churches of many denominations and hundreds of other Christian organizations around the world to help Christians grow in their faith and share the gospel message with their fellow citizens.

CaMPUS
CRUSaDE
FOR
CHRIST
INTERNaTIONAL

William R. Bright, President

Dear Baby,

Welcome to the world that was created by our loving and powerful heavenly Father, who loves you with a limitless and immeasurable unconditional love! You are God's latest creation, brought forth for His own plan and purpose, that you might know, serve, and enjoy Him forever.

Your arrival brings such happiness. You are so blessed that our Creator God sent you to such wonderful parents, who themselves have been especially chosen by God to be His special ministers to help tell the whole world about His love. His careful choice of parents for you is clear evidence that God must have a special love and plan for you.

Soon you will learn about God's greatest act of love for you—the greatest love story in history: God sent His own Son, Jesus Christ, to redeem you from this world which, though created beautiful and perfect, was marred by humans who disobeyed their Creator. When you hear and understand this story, be sure to accept God's great love for you.

In closing, I leave with you this special blessing that thousands of years ago God gave to His people, through Moses. I believe it still is in effect for God's people today: "The Lord bless you and keep you; the Lord make His face shine upon you, and be gracious to you; the Lord lift up His countenance upon you, and give you peace" (Num. 6:24–26, NKJV) for a long exciting, abundant, and fruitful life.

Yours for fulfilling the Great Commission in this generation,

Bill Bright

RAVI ZACHARIAS

In addition to being a great author, Ravi Zacharias has spoken in more than fifty countries, including the Middle East, Vietnam, and Cambodia (during the military conflict), and in numerous universities worldwide, notably Harvard and Princeton. He has addressed writers of the peace accord in South Africa, President Fujimoris' cabinet and parliament in Peru, and military officers at the Lenin Military Academy and the Center for Geopolitical Strategy in Moscow. He is well versed in the disciplines of comparative religions, cults, and philosophy and held the chair of Evangelism and Contemporary Thought at Alliance Theological Seminary for three-and-a-half years.

Ravi Zacharias International Ministries

OFFICE OF THE PRESIDENT

Dear Baby,

You did not choose to be born, but you have entered a world in which you will bear the consequences of your choices. You will hear many voices, be held in many arms, and marvel at many faces.

I wish I could say to you that those voices will all be filled with wisdom and those arms will never betray you and that those faces will always be there for you. The sad reality of life, dear one, is that disappointments carve deep furrows into our hearts and sometimes become the pathways through which our feelings will be channeled. Let not your heart be broken by humanity. Stay strong, for there is reason for confidence and hope.

For beyond the voices of men and women and children there is a still small voice—the voice of God. He has spoken and still speaks. I pray that early in your life somebody will read His Word to you, the Word that will make you wise unto salvation. I will pray that at every moment when you feel let down, the strong arms of God will uphold you. Take a good look at the cross, where His arms reached out to you. And I will pray that as the faces around you change or grow older or disappear, that you will see always the face of God in however a manner He will show Himself—for one day, His will be the voice; His will be the arms; His will be the face that you will enjoy forever.

Therefore, choose life—the life that He offers. His grace has made that possible, and may His grace guide you into truth.

Sincerely,

Ravi K. Zacharias

JOE WHITE

Joe White loves kids. And kids love Joe White. Joe has seen thousands and thousands of kids attend his Kanakuk and Kanakomo camps. He is a great speaker, motivator, and friend to all who have ever had the opportunity to spend any time with him.

KANAKUK-KANAKOMO KAMPS

Dear Baby,

Welcome to God's great big beautiful world! I know your mama and daddy are so glad you've come. They've been looking forward to this day for a long time now, and now that you're here, it's unanimous that it was well worth the wait.

Now that you've arrived, their lives will revolve around you. You'll be happy to know that they'll attend to all your needs. They'll feed you whenever you're hungry, night and day, and they'll change your diaper more times than any of you will ever be able to recall. And right away you'll recognize them not only by sound but also by their individual touch. They will thrill over the softness of your skin, the expressions on your face, and each little sound you make. Soon you'll smile and their wonder and amazement will continue to grow. The day you say "Mama" or "Dada" will be cause for celebration among all the friends and relatives.

Someday you'll recognize that the love they lavish upon you, little one, is but a small reflection of your heavenly Father's love for you. Hopefully your earthly parents will never disappoint you, but please know that you have a heavenly Father who will remain faithful. He is the giver of life, and your arrival here was planned by Him from the foundation of the earth. He loves you so much, dear baby, that He has made provision for you to live a joyful life here on this earth and then live forever with Him in heaven. You are His special child, a one-of-a-kind gift straight from His heart to all the people whose lives you will touch. Enjoy His goodness, and rest in His favor.

Much love,

Joe White

"Exciting Adventure In Christian Athletics"

James C. Dobson

James Dobson is uniquely qualified to write a letter to a baby. Dr. Dobson, a child psychologist, is the founder and president of Focus on the Family, a nonprofit organization that produces his internationally syndicated radio programs, heard on more than 2,900 radio stations. Dr. Dobson's books and video series have been some of the most praised and award-winning products of their type ever produced.

Dear Baby,

Welcome to planet Earth!

There are two messages your parents will be sending to you every day, and I hope you pick up on them very early in your life: (1) Your parents love you more than you can possibly understand (at least until you have children of your own); (2) Because they love you so much, they must teach you to obey them. That is the only way they can take care of you and protect you from things that might hurt you.

As you grow from childhood to adolescence, you will find the river of life getting a little rockier as you struggle to develop into an adult and deal with the unique pressures of the teenage years. Things are a lot harder on young people nowadays than they were when I was an adolescent, and, undoubtedly, the world will be an even harder place to grow up in when you reach junior high and high school. But you can make it, because your parents will have also introduced you to a wonderful Friend— Jesus Christ. The most important advice I can give you is to make friends with Jesus and remain friends with Him during the years ahead. He loves you and understands all of your needs and desires. He will be there to share your brightest days and your darkest nights. When you face the important issues of life (choosing a mate, selecting an occupation, etc.), He will guide your footsteps. He gave us that assurance in Proverbs 3:6 which says: "In all your ways acknowledge Him, and He shall direct your paths" (NKJV). What a comforting promise!

The final message I want to leave with you is: Be there! When you reach the end of your journey here on this planet, be there to meet your mother and father in heaven. They will be looking for you on that resurrection morning. Don't let anything deter you from keeping that appointment! Be there! This must be your ultimate objective in living.

I hope to meet you someday, Baby. If our paths don't cross this side of heaven, I'll be looking for you in that eternal city. By all means, be there!

Sincerely,

James C. Dobson, Ph.D.

Stephen Hicks

Stephen is part of the comedy team "Hicks and Cohagan." Stephen wrote the exact letter I knew he would—one with great wisdom, plus a pinch of humor to help it go down just a bit easier. His own battle with cancer is being fought with greater dignity and resolve than I could ever imagine. Stephen is a treasure in my life.

HICKS AND COHAGAN

Dear Little One,

So glad you're here! Life is already amazing, isn't it? I can just imagine your first thoughts as you look up at the faces of your admiring parents: *"Who are these bozos? And please tell me I didn't get his nose!"*

That will be the first of many amazing revelations. Before long, you will be forced to wear clothes that would make Dennis Rodman flinch. I won't even mention haircuts. And to insure your lifelong subservience, every moment of dorkiness will be preserved on film or videotape.

I should warn you that around the age of twelve or thirteen, the IQ of your parents (and virtually all adults) will inexplicably drop about forty points, during which time you will witness spontaneous looks of terror at your most innocent comments or plans. Sometimes you and your parents will lose the ability to communicate in English. Interaction will be reduced to an assortment of finely-nuanced shrugs, groans, sighs, and hand gestures. Hang in there. Almost overnight, if you are fortunate, you will rediscover the gift of family.

A word of advice about advice: Adults love to give advice. We rarely like to take it, however. But if we didn't burden you with all our insight and wisdom, how could we say "I told you so" later on when you ignore our advice! (But enough about my mother.)

It is natural and good to want to share our lives with each other. Even with all our uniqueness, we are on a common journey. Now, I am going to tell you a hard thing about the journey. You are living in a broken world where relationships, families, even people break. I wish it weren't so, dear one. My body has been broken with a disease called cancer. It is not fun. Yet life wants to teach me, even now.

So how will you live through broken moments in your life? Choose to be authentic—in other words, live your life truthfully, even when it's a struggle. Embrace your life, including moments of suffering—not to be a martyr, but to hear what life may wish to say to you. Let others share the journey. It will make the way easier. Choose to believe in something (or should I say Someone). Take chances; risk it.

In days hard or easy, be merciful and extravagant with forgiveness—it is one of our few unlimited resources. There is freedom in forgiveness. A writer I hope you will grow to love said, "The quality of mercy is not strained, it droppeth as the gentle rain from heaven upon the place beneath. It is twice blessed—it blesseth him that gives, and him that takes."

So travel lightly, with mercy as your map, grace your guide. If our journey here together is brief, don't despair. The time will surely come when we will sit together sharing stories of our amazing adventures. The heavens will echo with our laughter and joy.

Under His mercy,

Stephen Hicks

Tom Landry

From the moment Tom Landry began to coach the Dallas Cowboys, he was recognized as an innovator. He introduced the "flex" defense, restructured the "shotgun" offense, and guided the Cowboys to twenty consecutive winning seasons, eighteen playoff appearances, thirteen division championships, and five NFC titles for a record five Super Bowl appearances.

Tom Landry
Dallas, Texas

Dear Baby,

Welcome to the greatest country in the world. You will be growing up in a wonderful family that will be raising and loving you as a special gift from God.

My prayer for you is that you will grow in stature, always looking for the opportunity to serve those you come in contact with. The Lord will be a shining light for you to follow.

Our nation is special, and you can be a part of its continued growth.

Sincerely,

Alicia & Tom Landry

Alicia and Tom Landry

ROBERT SCHULLER

One of the most recognized men in America, Robert Schuller serves as the host of "The Hour of Power" television program. Broadcasting from his beautiful Crystal Cathedral, Dr. Schuller has been an encourager to millions.

ROBERT SCHULLER

Dear Baby,

Welcome to our world!

You have been given the most joyous, precious gift—the gift of life!

As you now begin your journey, you will have many joyous opportunities and adventures! Each day will be filled with new challenges and triumphs! Your opportunities are many, and you will be challenged in the pursuit of them.

Always remember that you can do anything you want to do and become anything you want to be—with God's help!

There is no one else in the world exactly like you!

You are the future!

My prayer is that you will forever be filled with hopes, dreams, and goals as you embark on the wonderful journey of life!

May you grow with God—He certainly loves you!

Robert H. Schuller

FAITH HILL
AND TIM MCGRAW

Faith and Tim are two of country music's biggest and brightest stars. Here is another example of someone who was genuinely excited to write a letter for this book. Faith wrote this letter while expecting their first child. It is truly a wonderful letter.

TOURS, INC.

Dear Baby,

As we prepare for your arrival, we reflect on the joy you have already brought into our lives just by knowing you are coming. There isn't a second that passes by that we do not imagine you in our arms.

God has blessed our lives with such a profound miracle in you. Our prayer is that, beyond any doubt, throughout your life you will find solace in the love that we will share with you. But most of all, we hope you will have the most peaceful feeling that exists, which comes from knowing that God's hand is on you to guide and direct you. He has always existed in you, and He will never leave your side. There is no greater lesson.

Welcome to the world, our sweet precious gift. We love and adore you.

Your mommy and daddy,

Faith Hill-McGraw and Tim McGraw

Pat McCaskey

Few sports franchises are as world renowned as the Chicago Bears. The Bears are an "institution" in Chicago. The team is owned and operated by the McCaskey family. In addition to his work as director of Community Involvement for the Chicago Bears, Pat McCaskey has found the time to write eleven books of stories and poems about faith, family, and sports.

CHICAGO BEARS

Dear Baby,

We are two championships behind the Packers, so please don't dawdle too long. We need your help!

We want to win championships with sportsmanship. We do good works quietly, for God's glory. We fear God and kryptonite. We are trying to keep the Bears going until the Second Coming. We work diligently and trust God for the results. Like the Magi who followed the great star, we go forward in faith.

We are grateful for at least the following: God created a wonderful world in six days; Jesus died for our sins, including my singing; when we need the Holy Spirit, He is there (He is even there when we think that we don't need Him).

We are hopeful that the world will not end until the Bears have the most championships. Instead of the Super Bowl Most Valuable Player saying that he is going to Disney World, he could say that he is going to heaven. After the presentation of the trophy, the rapture would be a great postgame show.

We want to play our games with cooperation that is like an Amish barnraising. We go to church and Bible study and have daily devotions. Our mandate is to love God and each other.

Halas Hall is a place of work and not a den of thieves. It is a halfway house to heaven. Instead of saying, "Please be quiet," we say, "Please become a mime." We give away the credit and we take the blame. We criticize privately and we praise publicly. Instead of singing as soloists, we sing as a chorus. We provide accountability and positive reinforcement for each other.

From William Bennett's book, *The Moral Compass*, we know that "Goethe once said that you must labor to possess what you have inherited. 'If we are not grateful for our gifts and opportunities, we are not likely to value them, and if we do not value them, we are not likely to work hard to preserve and improve them.'"

If you are not a Bear fan, don't be discouraged. Some of the greatest Christians started out as atheists.

Dominus vobiscum,

Pat McCaskey

Patrick McCaskey

Mike Yaconelli

Mike Yaconelli is the owner of Youth Specialties, a company specializing in training, seminars, conventions, videos, magazines, and other resource products for youth programs. YS has worked alongside youth workers of nearly every denomination and youth-serving organization in America and around the world.

Youth Specialties

Dear Little One,

    You have been brought into the world untamed. Childhood is the place where joy, laughter, imagination, and unpredictability run wild. The place where you never stop being astonished.

    May you never lose your childlikeness.

    May you never be tamed.

    Growing is a great and dangerous adventure. Live your life with childlike abandon so you can stay close to creativity, risk, and surprise. Don't be afraid of the unknown because mystery is where God hides. There is much to learn from failure, so fail magnificently. Play. Keep skipping. Keep dancing. Spend your life looking for the place "where the sidewalk ends."

    Fiercely protect the twinkle in your eye. Listen to how you were made because that is where the twinkle comes from. Revel in your "oddness," your God-given lopsidedness, your uniqueness. It is your differentness the world is longing to know. Listen to your calling—the place where your gifts live. Listen to the words of your own song because if you never hear your own song you will never be able to dance.

    Daydream. All-the-time-dream. Nothing is more sad than a person who has forgotten how to dream. Listen to your dreams, and they will always point you to the Dreamer.

    Make wonder your friend because gratitude, passion, and humility are always the result of such friendships. I must warn you, though, wonder is dangerous, gloriously dangerous. Life-giving dangerous.

    Learn to listen to the thin silence of God—whose whispering voice can drown out the blaring voices of our culture who say that what you do is more important than who you are, winning is more important than losing, getting is more important than giving, and busyness is more important than silence. Those are the voices of boredom and dullness. Ignore them. Seek God's voice instead because if you do, you will hear a wondrously terrifying truth: life is found where God is.

    When you are older, if you are lucky, someone will read to you *The Chronicles of Narnia*. There, in the pages of *The Lion, The Witch and the Wardrobe* you will meet Aslan, "the King of the wood and the son of the great Emperor-Beyond-the-Sea"—the same one, by the way, who spoke you into existence. Then, if you are really lucky, you will meet that same Aslan in the pages of your life, and the mad chase will begin.

    May your life be one long romp with God so that when your days are over, you will lie panting in the sun, no longer feeling in the least tired or hungry or thirsty.

    Mike Yaconelli
    Lifetime Youthworker

National Youth Workers Convention ♦ National Resource Seminar for Youth Workers ♦ YS Books & Videos ♦ Online Services
Edge TV ♦ *Youthworker* journal ♦ *Youthworker Update* newsletter

Amy Grant

Amy's career has been amazing. With more than twenty-two million records sold, she is respected in both the contemporary Christian and mainstream markets. She is a gifted singer/songwriter and a very special friend. Her letter is shared from her son Matt's baby book.

Once a mom, always a mom … And so, here is the letter written to my first child born July 7, 1987.

For many years I've looked forward to starting a family of my own. I've pictured a child in my arms, tried to imagine every feature of the face that would one day form inside of me. Well, now you are almost here, Little One.

My dream is that we will grow in this new relationship together. I will try to always love you with an open embrace, holding you when you need my comfort, yet continually training you for the day when you will leave this home to begin your own.

Every day I anticipate the ways that, through your eyes, I will discover the mysteries of this world again. I hope to be your biggest fan, the happiest laugher at your jokes, your dependable confidant, and your constant supporter in prayer.

For you I wish a long and peaceful life—never driven by some unspoken "ought," but a life filled with joy as you learn to appreciate the simple beauty of the time that God has given you on this planet. I pray that you will know always that there is nothing you will ever do that will make me stop loving you. I am so proud and honored that God has given you to me. I love you.

Orel Hershiser

One of major league baseball's most respected and awarded pitchers, Orel Hershiser now plays for the Cleveland Indians. He holds the major league single-season record for most consecutive scoreless innings—fifty nine! He is respected as much for his kindness and genuine likeability as he is for his outstanding play.

Dear Baby,

Today is a day that cannot be equaled because you were born! What a miracle. You are very important to God—so much that He is aware of the smallest details about you, even to the most intricate part. He created you!

My prayer for you as you grow and develop is that you will understand what a special gift you are to your family and to all who will know you. I pray for your parents to be able to instill within you the truths of God's Word. I pray also that they will be able to lead you to know Jesus Christ as your personal Savior one day. As you mature from that point I would also ask that God would use you to help others come to know Christ as well. Our world needs people like you—those unashamed to let others know who He is.

This world is a tougher place to grow up in than it used to be. Don't let that stop you from believing what God's Word says about living your life. Stand tall, and always hope and believe in what is right. Love others, and care about their needs before your own. "Let your light shine before men, that they may see your good deeds and praise your Father in heaven" (Matt. 5:16, NKJV).

In His grip,

Orel Hershiser

Orel Hershiser

Robert A. Briner

Bob Briner is the president of ProServe Television, the company that made international tennis a spectator sport for TV. Currently, ProServe produces the U.S. Open and French Open tennis tournaments along with a host of other events. ProServe also provides agency representation for many of today's top athletes in major league sports. Despite his many accomplishments, those privileged to spend time with Bob instantly feel their own worth. His book, *Roaring Lambs*, greatly affected the way many of us think. His "gentle plan to radically change our world" has had an incredible impact on thousands.

ROBERT A. BRINER

Dear Baby,

What a joy it is to write to you. I do it in celebration of all you can be to your family, to our country, and, most importantly, to God's kingdom.

As I think about my message to you, I am thankful to know that many others who care about you and your parents will also be writing to you, and that you will receive words much more meaningful and profound than any I could ever pen. Knowing this gives me the freedom to concentrate on a message that I hope will help bring you countless hours of gladness while preparing you to do great things.

My prayer for you is that even as you first learn to speak, among your most frequent expressions will be, "Sing me a song" and "Tell me a story." My hope is that music and reading will play important, enriching, and empowering roles in your life. Music and language are such wonderful gifts from your heavenly Father. Make sure you use them to the fullest. Enjoy them to the fullest. Let them help you grow to be great in character and humble in spirit—become a roaring lamb.

Most prominent among the songs you will hear and sing and among the stories you will hear and read will, I hope, be ones about Jesus. He is the most beautiful song and the most powerful word.

Have a wonderful life!

Robert A. Briner

MARY FISHER

Mary Fisher was catapulted into the spotlight as one of the keynote speakers at the 1988 Republican Presidential Convention. Her opening statement, "My name is Mary Fisher and I have AIDS," sent a message to all America and to the world. This disease was indeed among us and had to be reckoned with. Mary's resolve and determination has led her to speak to groups throughout the world about this growing problem in our society. She is a great inspiration.

MARY FISHER

My Dear Baby,

Today you have met your new family for the very first time. All the attention you are receiving has probably left you exhausted, but I'm sure you will become accustomed to all the kissing and rocking and peeking over the edge of the crib. They love you madly, even though this is only your first day with them. And it's a love that is certain to grow and grow and grow. I know, because like your new mom and dad, I am the proud parent of an adopted child.

Your mom and dad have been awaiting your arrival for what seemed to them an endless accounting of day adding to day. When focused so completely on wanting a child to be part of your family the days can seem very long indeed. Now their prayers have been answered and their wishes fulfilled. It's a big role for such a little person to fill, but I'm certain you will be perfect in the part. I've seen your gentle smile and looked into those big blue eyes, so I know you will understand and be very kind when Mom and Dad coo at you just a bit too loudly or find your every accomplishment to be far more stupendous than you know it is. They will eventually get the hang of this parenting thing . . . but they need you to help them along the way!

When they first heard the news about their new baby, your parents weren't sure who you would be. We all knew, however, that you were going to be a very, very special addition to their lives. I tried to explain to them how their hearts would be filled to overflowing when they held you for the first time, but they had to experience the joy of you to understand what my words couldn't adequately express.

Thank you for the smile you share so freely . . . for that deep, rippling gurgle that escapes just behind the smile . . . and thank you especially for the spark you have added to Mom's blue eyes each time she holds your chubby fingers in her hand and for the dimple that caresses Dad's face whenever he peeks around the corner into your room. Being a gift is a pretty wonderful thing.

Welcome to the world. Welcome to your new family. And welcome to the love that has only today begun to grow.

With many hugs and kisses,

Mary Fisher,

Pat Robertson

M. G. "Pat" Robertson is an internationally renowned religious broadcaster whose perspective on world events and commitment to humanitarianism are respected by millions around the world. He is the founder of The Christian Broadcasting Network, Inc., Regent University, and Operation Blessing International Relief and Development Corporation. He is seen by millions daily as the host of "The 700 Club."

The Christian Broadcasting Network Inc.

Pat Robertson
CHAIRMAN OF THE BOARD
CHIEF EXECUTIVE OFFICER

Dear Baby,

I welcome you into the world. This world can be a place of laughter, of joy, of love, of tenderness. It can be a world of hope, and opportunity, and freedom, and blessing. Unfortunately those of my generation have not worked as hard as we might to keep it that way.

Instead, you may be facing a world of hatred and violence, racial strife, and the tearing apart of the home. In your school you may encounter those who want to destroy your body through drugs or promiscuity, or physically assault you with dangerous weapons. So I counsel you to do everything you can to seek out the good and the lovely, and to resist those who would trample on the rights of others.

How will you know what to do? Who will take you by the hand to care for you and nurture you while you are growing up? First, I would advise you to look to your parents. Honor them, obey them, and let them teach you what is good and right. Beyond that, and even more importantly, I would advise you as soon as you are old enough to commit your life to Jesus Christ. Receive Him as your Savior. Let Him be your friend, your guide, and your Lord.

I can't promise you what the future will hold for you, or for this great country we now live in, but I can assure you that Jesus Christ holds the future, and if He holds you, you have nothing to fear from what may lie ahead in your life.

Sincerely,

Pat Robertson

Scott O'Grady

On June 2, 1995, the world held its breath—Air Force Captain Scott O'Grady had been shot down over war-torn Bosnia. He eluded the Bosnian Serbs for six days, relying on his survival training and his deep faith in God. I will never forget those first images of a smiling Scott O'Grady after his rescue. Likewise I will never forget the dignity with which he payed tribute to his rescuers and his God. Scott is a true American hero and a wonderful friend.

Dear Baby,

Welcome to the world! You have an amazing adventure ahead of you. Full of joy and wonder, hardships and challenge. You will never know what is around the next corner or what might happen the next day. Life is definitely never boring. Embrace it and cherish it for what it is: a gift. For life is truly beautiful, and every day, a blessing.

At times life can be very confusing in the world we live in, a world where everyone is searching, searching for success and happiness. In your journey for the same, just remember that the following doesn't come once you reach a destination; true success and happiness are found in the journey. To be happy is to find it within yourself, being thankful for who you are and content with what you have today and not always looking to be happy tomorrow or some-time in the future. Once you understand this and fully take it to heart, you will be successful in your adventure.

You will learn that the only truly important things are your relationships. The relationship you have with God and learning what is eternal within you is what life is all about. And the love that you share with your family and friends is the most important part of your life here on earth—these relationships will carry on even when your adventure here ends; these relationships are where love and happiness flourish. So when all is said and done and it comes time for you to look back on the adventure you are just now beginning, a time to reflect and to see if you were successful in your life, ask yourself this one question: Was I successful in my relationships? If you can say yes, then you will have lived a life full of love, happiness, and meaning. And it is this that I truly wish for you.

Life is beautiful.

God Bless!

Scott O'Grady, Captain

Wesley K. Stafford

A broad range of experience has convinced Dr. Wesley Stafford that people are a priceless resource. Wess spent fifteen years with Compassion International, both overseas and at its headquarters, before becoming its president in early September 1993. Specializing in Christian child development, Compassion has aided children throughout the world with food, educational opportunities, and hope.

Dear Baby,

I don't know you, yet I feel like I do. You see, I have spent my life working to help children. I'm one of the lucky ones who have had the opportunity to hold children from all over the world on my lap, to be hugged by them, and to learn from them. Many of them have been very poor, some very sick, some even dying. But all of them want basically the same thing.

You are coming into a world that is wonderful and harsh at the same time. God, your heavenly Father, made this beautiful creation to nourish us and for us to take care of. You'll find lots of things in this world that are really neat and interesting. You'll find joy in watching a butterfly flutter just above your outstretched hands, in wrestling with a puppy or a kitten, and in planting your first seed and seeing it grow. All of this was made for you because you are special and God loves you.

I know your parents will love you and try their best to provide for you. But sometimes that doesn't happen. Sometimes families don't do everything right or can't do everything they need to, and kids get hurt. That makes me sad, and I think that makes God sad too. I told you before that I think I know what kids want. Whether poor or rich, they want to be loved and to feel special and to have a family where they are safe and cared for. That's how God meant it to be. But God knows that the world is messed up. And God cares. He cares so much that He even sent His very own Baby to help us out—to change our lives and stop us from messing up so much. As you grow up, you'll realize that you mess up, too, and that you need help. God will be there in those times.

Don't ever believe that life is about what you have, or what you wear, or what you look like. Whether you are rich or poor, you have some great gifts. You have life itself. You have a family that loves you. And you know you are special in God's eyes. No matter what the situation, you always have something to offer—a smile, an encouraging word, an act of kindness. Don't be selfish with the gifts God has given to you. Learn to love and learn to forgive.

I love you even though I don't know you. You have a whole life ahead of you. Remember that life is for living; people are for loving; things are for giving. It won't all be easy. Some days will be like an easy walk through the daisies, and others will feel like you are clinging onto the side of a cliff by your fingernails. But life is a great adventure. Make sure you get the right Guidebook. Travel with good companions. Take some rests along the way. Enjoy the journey, and I hope to see you when it's all over!

Wishing you joy in your journey,

Wesley K. Stafford
President, Compassion International

Jim Bakker

Jim Bakker has gone from PTL ministries, to prison, to a very simple, secluded life on a North Carolina farm. I appreciate his willingness to share this very personal and wonderful letter that he wrote to his own grandson.

JIM BAKKER

Dear Baby James,

The first time I saw you was just minutes after you were born. The doctor had put a little hat on your head to keep you warm. As I peeked in the room, there you were, so cute looking, like you were ready to go out and meet the world. What a wonderful surprise when your mom told me they had named you after me!

When your mommy and daddy brought you home, we were all living together in a great big log house. I got to hold you a lot, and you and I would snuggle up and you would go fast asleep.

"Paw Paw Jim" was going through a very hard time when you were born, and you gave me a reason to live. The day before I went away to prison, you and your mommy and daddy came and spent the night with me in my hotel room. I took care of you all night and fed you your baby formula. It meant so much to me that you were there with me.

All through the years I was in prison, I had your picture with me in every cell. Sometimes, when things got real bad, I would hold your picture close to my eyes, blotting out everything around me except your wonderful face.

I wish I could tell you how much you mean to me. Perhaps when you are grown, I will be able to tell you more, but if not, I hope you will find this letter and know how much "Paw Paw Jim" loves you and thanks God for you.

Baby James, I love you!

Love,

Paw Paw Jim

Paw Paw Jim

Ara Parseghian

Ara Parseghian is one of the most respected men to ever coach college football. As the coach for Notre Dame, he groomed several All-Americans, including Joe Theisman, Joe Montana, and John Huarte. With a record of ninety-five victories, seventeen losses, and four ties, Ara is one of the winningest coaches in Notre Dame history—second only to Knute Rockne.

Ara Parseghian
MEDICAL RESEARCH FOUNDATION
A GOAL FOR LIFE

Dear Baby,

I am writing this at the twilight of my life as you begin the sunrise of your exciting new journey.

During my lifetime I have seen the advent of jet aircraft, television, computers, and many medical, technical, and scientific developments. Yes, in my time we put a man on the moon. It has been a time when immigrants like my French mother and Armenian father became privileged to come to America, become citizens, and enjoy the fruits of a free society. Early on, my parents recognized the importance of an education. They sacrificed to make sure that my brother, sister, and I completed our college degrees.

My love of sports led me to the coaching profession. It was exciting and challenging with the highs and lows of competing. One of the great lessons I learned by participation and coaching was how to handle adversity. You will experience disappointments and setbacks as you move through your lifespan. The mark of your success will be your ability to handle these adverse circumstances and bounce back to meet these challenges square in the eye.

Let me tell you a story about facing the greatest challenge of my life. Three of my grandchildren were diagnosed as having a terrible disease that is progressively and relentlessly destroying their bodies and minds. The affliction is called Niemann–Pick Type C. One day when you are old enough, you will read in the history books about our team's victory over this horrible disease, achieved through teamwork, determination, and bouncing back from adversity.

Prepare yourself with good health habits and extended education: learn from your life experiences. In this way you will face the challenges of life's journey.

My best wishes,

Ara Parseghian

Ara Parseghian

Rich Mullins

Rich's incredible depth and great sense
of humor are played out in this letter.
Rich's songs like "Awesome God,"
"Sometimes Step by Step," and "Sing
Your Praise to the Lord" and others
have become standards.

Dear Baby,

The place is a mess, but help yourself to whatever good you find. Everyone wishes we could have gotten everything cleaner and safer for you—though a good many of us are beginning to suspect that much of the mess and danger you face is in those very wishes. So, take with a grain of salt all of those anxieties and ambitions we'll doubtless project onto you. And do us the favor of looking at us with your perfectly blank stare so we can see what we look like to someone whose sight is empowered by purity, not impaired by experience. Your stay here, like all of ours, is so brief. Make the most of your time, and try to put things back at least as nicely as you found them.

Rich Mullins

Rich Mullins

Art Linkletter

Known to millions whose lives are brightened by his humor and geniality, Art Linkletter reached fame from the bleakest of beginnings. At birth, little A. G. Kelley was abandoned. He was adopted by the Linkletter family and went to work at a very early age to help with expenses. He worked his way through college and developed a liking for radio, which led to a phenomenal career in broadcasting. "People Are Funny" and "House Party" were two of the longest-running shows in program history.

Art Linkletter

Dear Baby,

Congratulations and best wishes on your safe arrival. You have just arrived in the midst of the greatest and most exciting period in the history of mankind. You will be confronted in the next eighty years with constant change and challenges of every imaginable sort. The first couple of years will see your brain grow and develop at a faster pace and with greater significance to your future life than at any other time of your life. You will discover that living is an exciting, confusing, rewarding, frustrating, bewildering, unending condition that will be filled with surprises and require a constant struggle on your part to have self-esteem built on a solid foundation of positive thinking.

You will live longer, probably, than 95 percent of the world population who were born before you because you are arriving in the midst of a longevity revolution. In the last one hundred years the average child born in the U.S. has been given almost thirty years of additional life. If you had been born one hundred years ago, you could expect to live to be forty-seven years of age. Since you have just been born, you can now expect to live to be seventy-seven. Think of what this means. You will be healthier, wiser, better informed, and be given opportunities for a number of careers that would have been impossible just a few years ago. It is up to you to make the most of these years. First, you must definitely plan to go to college and get at least a master's degree, preferably in communications and information. Secondly, your education will never cease because everything is changing so fast and so constantly that you will never be able to "rest on your oars" but will have to constantly adapt to new conditions and new opportunities.

Remember that life is what happens to you while you are making other plans, so make up your mind to accept change and avoid comfortable ruts.

Finally, remember that things turn out best for the people who make the best of the way things turn out.

Best of luck!

Cordially,

Art Linkletter

Greg Laurie

Greg Laurie is senior pastor of Harvest Christian Fellowship in Riverside, California. He began his pastoral ministry at age nineteen by leading a Bible study of thirty people. Today, that small group has grown into a church of twelve thousand people, making it one of the largest churches in America. Greg's Harvest Crusades have affected people all over the country.

Dear Baby,

First of all, welcome! I'm glad you're here. There are a lot of things you are going to discover in life that are important in the years ahead. When you're younger you're going to look forward to getting older. Especially when you reach the those pre-teen years. Time at first will seem to pass so slowly (especially in school!) but as you get older it will go by faster and faster. Then when you hit your late thirties and fourtiess you will remember those days of youth as the "good old days." So just enjoy it each day at a time.

There is something, however, that I want to tell you that you need to know. It's about your real purpose in life. In fact, if you learn this while you're still young, your life will be so much richer and fuller. Here it is: You were born to know God—not just as a distant deity but as your Creator, Lord, Savior, and, yes, your Friend. You were also born to glorify Him.

Many things in life will pull you this way and that.But just remember: To know God and glorify Him, that's what really matters in life. But there's this big wall that separates us from God. It's called sin. Sin is all those bad things we do (and some bad things we don't even know we've done), but God loved you so much that He sent His Son, Jesus Christ, to this earth to die for every sin you will ever commit. If you turn from your sins and follow Jesus, you will enter into this wonderful friendship with God!

Did I mention that His plans for your future are incredible? He says to you, "For I know the plans I have for you, says the Lord. They are plans for good and not for evil, to give you a future and a hope. In those days when you pray, I will listen. You will find me when you seek me, if you look for me in earnest" (Jer. 29:11–13, TLB)

So God bless you, Baby. May you know and glorify God and live a wonderful life!

Your friend,

Greg Laurie

MICHAEL MEDVED

Michael Medved is a nationally recognized film critic, best-selling author, and network television personality. He served as cohost (with Jeffrey Lyons) of "Sneak Previews," a half-hour movie review show aired on more than 240 stations through the Public Broadcasting System.

In addition to his columns and reviews, Mr. Medved's comments on media and society have appeared in the *Wall Street Journal*, the *New York Times*, the *Los Angeles Tribune*, and many other publications. He has also appeared regularly as a guest on ABC's "Nightline," "The Oprah Winfrey Show," "The Today Show," and many other television shows.

Dear Baby,

While you're busy entering this world, you may be too busy to look around and count your blessings, so let me remind you of your own extraordinary good fortune.

You're joining the human adventure at a golden moment in world history.

Never before have so many of earth's people lived under governments of their own choosing, with fundamental freedoms that their ancestors could scarcely imagine. The ancient enemies of humankind—disease, starvation, tyranny—have not yet been conquered, but everywhere they are in retreat. Just think: only one century ago, your chances of reaching adulthood would have been less than 50 percent. Today, if you avoid senselessly destructive personal choices (particularly involving drugs or violence) the likelihood is overwhelming that you'll live to see children of your own.

But you're not only arriving at a point in time that makes you the envy of all past centuries, you're also lucky enough to join a nation that is the envy of all the earth. It won't take long before babies in every corner of the globe, born the same moment you are, will begin yearning to make their way to America. And who can blame them? Your country is the only one on the planet with dreams and decency to match the incomparable grandeur of its landscape.

Soon after you arrive, you may be exposed to forces that might try to blind you to your uniquely favored status, but never surrender to cynicism or whining. Don't give in to the allure of self-pity, or a phony nostalgia that glorifies some other time or place while ignoring the magnificence of what we have. The only way to appreciate the present and feel confident about the future is to come to terms truthfully with the past. When you do, you'll see how much you owe to those who came before you and helped create the dazzling opportunities you'll enjoy.

My favorite uncle, may he rest in peace, used to tell me that even if I worked every day of my life to try to serve the United States, I could never repay the debt that my family owes to this great country. The same is true for you. An acknowledgment of that debt isn't enslaving—it's liberating, in the sense that facing the truth is always liberating.

By the same token, even if you express your appreciation to God every day of your life, you'd never be able to repay your debt to this gracious Creator—who's prepared the sights, sounds, smells, tastes, friendships, challenges, and revelations that will soon flood your tender senses and face your precious soul. The only way to approach that debt is to say "thank you," which should be the first thought you feel and understand, even before you can pronounce the words.

Those of us who've already been on this earth for some time hope to travel with you a while longer, and we offer you a hearty "welcome aboard!"

Yours, with love,

Michael Medved

DONNY OSMOND

Fame found Donny Osmond in 1963 at the age of five. The next decade of his life introduced him to superstardom. Through TV, film, and records, Donny is known to millions and millions. In 1992 Donny was offered, and accepted, the starring role in Andrew Lloyd Webber's *Joseph and the Amazing Technicolor Dreamcoat*. He has achieved tremendous success during the five years he has portrayed Joseph.

Donny Osmond

Dear Baby,

Welcome to this world! It's an exciting place. You are going to have a great time here as you grow up with all kinds of things to experience, places to see, and friends to make. There are a lot of good things in this world, but, unfortunately, there are some not-so-good things as well, so be very careful. Trust those who love you unconditionally.

As you grow up, there will be many friends who you will come in contact with who will try to influence your thinking and behavior. Always choose friends that make you want to be a better person. As you climb that so-called, "ladder of life," those friends should be the kind of people who help pull you up that ladder, not pull you down.

Have a firm conviction of your values and standards because there will be times when people will challenge you and tease you and make fun of those beliefs. If you're not firmly rooted in your convictions, there is a chance that you may go against what you know to be true, just for the sake of acceptance by those who may be considered popular at the time. This will only lead you to heartache and sorrow in the long run.

You can be as successful as you want to be. So many people believe that luck is the biggest factor in achieving success. I live by a different philosophy. When I was a teenager, I recorded a song called "Life Is Just What You Make It," and I really believe it too. Success comes when "opportunity meets preparedness." I worked hard when I was growing up to achieve my success. The value of hard work is something that my parents instilled in me at a young age, and I'm grateful for it. You can never replace hard work. People will respect you for it.

Choosing your goals in life will be exciting. There are so many things you can be successful at. I remember a quote from a man whom I respect a lot. His name was David O. McKay. He said, "No other success can compensate for failure in the home." I was blessed to have a good family. Some aren't as fortunate. But you can have a good strong family life by learning what integrity, honesty, and selflessness mean. This will be the foundation of a peaceful life for you—one that is full of happiness and contentment, especially in those times of distress. Your family is the single most important source of strength there is when times get rough. Never neglect them for the sake of praise of the world. At times it may seem like the family life is not very cool or appealing, and the worldly ways are a better and much more exciting alternative, but never underestimate the long-lasting joy that comes from a loving family and your relationships with them.

Last but not least, never forget that there is a purpose for your being here on this earth. There is a plan. I firmly believe this with all my heart. You have a loving heavenly Father who knows you and wants you to return to Him, and you have a Savior who atoned for all the sins of the world, who gave us all the opportunity to return to their presence. What peace this statement gives, especially in a world that doesn't offer very much peace.

In closing, my father always said, "Anything worth doing is worth doing well." Always remember, though, that the most important work you will ever do will be within the walls of your own home.

Have a wonderful life,

Donny Osmond

Carman

Carman is one of the most dynamic artists in Christian music. He has had incredible success, including stadium concerts with more than seventy thousand people in attendance. He has sold more than seven million records, earning an impressive seven gold records. Carman has also achieved four gold and two platinum awards for his music videos.

Hey Junior,

Welcome to Boot Camp. I know there's gonna be a lot of hoopla made about your arrival, your accomplishments, and your legacy, but it's all preparation for life beyond "the tomb." But right now you're just trying to get a grip on life beyond "the womb," so let me give you some workable advice.

Life here on planet "E" can really be quite enjoyable if you have a solid relationship with the One who invented it. You see, kid, it's not about what you know but who you know, whether it's politics, entertainment, or eternal security. As soon as you possibly can, get to know the One who spoke the worlds into existence; the One who said, "Let there be light" and it showed up; the One who developed the whole concept of man's existence; and the One who knows how you tick better than you ever will. Get to know Jesus personally. The whole quality of your life here and through eternity pivots on that one thing: salvation through Him.

And don't forget the instruction manual, the blueprint, the map, the directions—man, don't forget the Bible. Once you learn how to read, it'll show you how to live life to the absolute maximum.

Oh yeah, and finally, you're gonna have to learn to forgive folks real quick. There's this guy named Adam who jacked everybody up years ago (read Genesis) and this thing called sin came into the human race. (Trust me, you'll hear a lot about that later.) People mess up a whole lot, but they're still good people, so please, please, please learn to forgive and let it go. And then there's a lot of evil in this world that will make you want to quit and end it all. Just remember: with the Spirit of God and the Word of God in you, you'll be a greater threat to the evil of your day than the evil of your day is a threat to you.

See you in heaven, kid!

Carman

Joe Gibbs

Joe Gibbs was head coach for the Washington Redskins for twelve victorious seasons. Gibbs became the tenth-winningest coach in the history of the NFL by leading the Redskins to 140 victories, including three Super bowl wins in four appearances.

After his retirement as head coach, he pursued his second love, NASCAR racing. Just one year after making their debut on the NASCAR Winston Cup Circuit, the Joe Gibbs Racing Team won the 1993 Daytona 500 with driver Dale Jarrett.

Dear Baby,

Welcome to this beautiful gift from God—life!

As you enter this world, you will hear many different voices telling you many different directions you should go with your life. From the time I was very small, growing up in the hills of North Carolina, I was blessed with a grandmother and mother who instilled in me the desire to read and study the Bible. With their encouragement, along with my pastor at our church, I found what I know to be the truth. Think about it: the Bible was written by thirty-five authors over a period of fifteen hundred years, and so far, everything about it, from beginning to end, has been perfect. Can you imagine how difficult a task that would be? As a coach, I've had to call plays from a press box by telling an assistant coach who told a player who eventually told the quarterback. It's amazing they ever got the message right! God created Adam and Eve, and you and me, for a purpose. He wants to have a relationship with us. That is why, at age nine, I trusted Christ as my Savior and Lord.

As I grew older, I had ideas and dreams like everyone else. I wanted to be happy and successful. The world will tell you to pursue money, materialism, and fame. I began to see a different plan, God's plan. God's plan was not based on money, position, or winning football games. God was only concerned that I have a right relationship with Him. I took the long road, but what I found was that success and happiness were by-products of a life given over to God. It seems I had to learn that lesson more than once. And in many ways, I'm still learning it.

Early in life I encourage you to know that God loves you and that He has a plan for your life. Acknowledge that God loved you so much that He sent His only Son to die on the cross for your sins. Learn of Him and understand Him. Invite Him to come into your heart and take control of your life. Ask Him to guide you into the person He wishes you to be. Our greatest sin is not realizing the breadth and scope of His love for us and not yielding to His lordship.

This gift of life will be a great adventure for you as you walk with God. God bless you!

Sincerely,

Joe Gibbs

CHARLES COLSON

Charles (Chuck) Colson, former special counsel to President Richard Nixon, served seven months in prison for Watergate-related offenses.

In 1976 he founded Prison Fellowship Ministries, an international organization that ministers to prisoners, their families, and victims of crime. He is the author of several books and is the voice of "Breakpoint," a daily radio commentary that offers a Christian perspective on news and trends, which is carried on more than 350 stations nationwide.

Dear Baby,

Welcome to this big world, little one, and welcome to one of the greatest families this world has to offer.

If God has given you even a portion of the talents your family possesses, you are most blessed. And yet He has made you a very special person with your very own identity. Your parents will see that as you pass through various stages. You will find your own faith in God and assurance of His love as you grow older, but your first knowledge of Him will come as you experience it firsthand through those who love you.

So grow strong, little one, in physical, mental, and spiritual strength, and God will be with you every step of the way.

Yours in His service,

Charles W. Colson

Pat Boone

Pat Boone has been in the entertainment business since his teenage years
in Tennessee, when he performed on
the "Ted Mack Amateur Hour." He has
sold more than forty-four million
records worldwide. In addition to
recording, Pat is an actor and a published author.

PAT BOONE
■ ENTERPRISES

Hi little kid!

You look just like your Creator.

In fact, you are made in His image, and He loves you. He molded and shaped you, breathed His own Holy breath into you, and gave you life.

In fact, He loves you so much that He took on human form, was born just like you, just as defenseless and precious and wonderful as you are, and grew into a mature human being, just like you will.

And then He died, willingly, to save your soul and give you a chance to live with Him in yet another world, throughout eternity. Isn't that great news?

See, He knew that you, like all of us, would make all sorts of mistakes in this life, and that sooner or later you would forfeit that eternal destiny He had planned for you. So, knowing you could never restore what was broken, He did it for you, in advance—with His own blood and bone, flesh' and spirit.

So, little creature, enjoy every breath, every minute of this existence, if you can. And just know that when you do eventually feel yourself separated from your loving Creator, that He's already provided the only avenue of return—through His own Son Jesus. And Jesus once looked exactly like yc

Pat Boone

Wayne Watson

Wayne Watson is a well-known and respected artist in contemporary Christian music. He has received multiple Dove Awards and has twice been nominated for a Grammy. His compassion and concern for others and his awareness of the challenges and rewards of family life have provided a unique foundation for his music.

To Baby,

Hello! Wow, we're all glad you're finally here. That entry was a fizzle traumatic, huh! Well, people are gonna do everything for you for a few years now, so enjoy it!

Your mom and dad really are stunned at how much they love you. I can't imagine what they would do if anyone tried to harm you. You have suddenly become their highest priority on the planet. Your needs are the first thing on their list. You will get used to being loved so much, but I hope you never take it for granted.

By the way, your parents are learning a lot about God right now. They never realized how much they were loved. They're learning the many parallels between their love for you and God's great love for them. One startling difference, though, is that one day, you'll grow up and you won't be so dependent on your parents. Growing spiritually, on the other hand, will take you to a place where you lean more and more on your Lord.

There's a lot for you to learn, but hey, don't rush it. It really doesn't matter if you're reading by the time you're three! I pray that you'll enjoy your childhood and that all through your life you'll keep a childlike faith. I pray, too, that you'll know His grace—that by His mercy He doesn't treat any of us the way we really deserve to be treated. And finally, I'm praying for you to have a heart of gratitude. Thankfulness all through your years will help dispel much bitterness and resentment. Gratitude for God's blessings can calm you in an angry world. Make it a lifetime habit to stop from time to time and look around at all the wonderful things God has done.

Okay, enough grown-up talk for now. You're only gonna be awake for another . . . hey, wake up! . . . No, you sleep now. There's a great lifetime ahead.

Your friend,

Wayne Watson

Frank E. Peretti

Peretti novels like *This Present Darkness*, *Piercing the Darkness,* and *The Oath* have opened the genre of Christian fiction to millions of people. At the same time, Frank's *Cooper Kid Adventure* series has become a mainstay for young readers. Frank is simply a great storyteller.

Dear Baby,

Welcome to our world, already in progress. The rest of us have been here quite a while, dreaming, struggling, often quarreling, making this world the way it is. We've done some things right and some things wrong, performed deeds both admirable and despicable, and the net result is where you'll be spending your life. Sorry about the wrinkles and blemishes here and there. We were hoping to have things in better shape.

But now it's your world too. You now have a hand in this ongoing project. You're a part of us, a soon-to-be doer of good or evil, your choice.

I pray you will choose to do good, to do the right thing—even if it hurts. The choices you make can reach far into the future, affecting not only your own life but the lives of those you love and even those you will never meet. And some choices you can never undo.

To know what is good, you must know God; and to know God, you must know Jesus. Make every effort to find Him, know Him, and serve Him. Learn His ways and follow them. Trust Him more than you trust your own feelings, and let His wisdom guide you. The best convictions of the godless can shift and betray; the convictions of the godly cannot be shaken and will serve them well all their lives.

Before complaining about the darkness in this world, remember that it's people who make this world what it is, and now you're one of them. Decide to make a difference. If someone needs a touch of kindness, let it come from you. Never hold back your smile; somebody needs it. Be ready to forgive the faults, and praise the good you find in people. Share what you have; give what you can.

Above all, place your life in God's hands and trust Him to order it. Many years have passed since I was where you are now, enough to prove to me that it is safe and altogether wise to trust God, for He is faithful.

I love you, child. I wish you a wonderful life.

Frank E. Peretti

Frank E. Peretti

LUCI FREED

Luci is the director of our local Crisis Pregnancy Support Center in Nashville, Tennessee. Luci has been there for hundreds of women who have found themselves frightened and confused with an unexpected pregnancy. She has also led hundreds of women and families through post-abortion counseling. Luci is one of the most gifted women I know, and I knew her amazing love for children would prompt a great letter.

CRISIS PREGNANCY SUPPORT CENTER

Dear Baby,

Welcome to the world. A lot of people who love you have been anxiously awaiting your arrival. Get to know them and let them love you as much as possible. You will need all that love and more as a foundation to build on.

God is excited about your arrival on earth too! You are very precious and valuable to Him. You see, He planned before the beginning of time for you to come to earth at exactly this time and place. God created you, knows you through and through, and has a very special purpose that only you can accomplish.

Along with that special purpose, He also wants you to love Him and let Him love you—then give that love to others. It is like a circle. Everybody down here needs a lot of love. You will notice that most people are scrambling everywhere trying to get it. We are pretty mixed up about what love really is. God is Love, and He is the only love that satisfies the soul.

I hope you will spend your days here being loved by Him and giving that love away. It is the only thing that matters in the end. While you are loving, being loved, and giving, He will show you that certain "area" where you can be most effective when you grow up. You will just know. He will be beside you and in you and with you then—just like He is right now.

Welcome to the world. Everybody in the grandstands of heaven and a lot here on earth are standing up to cheer. Here you come!! Hurrah!!

May you always know the stands are full of cheers, and it is all for you.

Luci Freed

GLORIA GAITHER

Gloria is a wife, mother, grandmother, author, lyricist, teacher, and speaker! She has authored twelve books and has written lyrics to more than six hundred songs. She is the writer of such classics as "Because He Lives," "The King is Coming," and "Something Beautiful." With her husband, Bill Gaither, and the Gaither Trio, she has recorded more than sixty albums.

Dear Little One,

I wish great things for you. So many gifts would I give you—gifts that you will never outgrow and treasures that will not be destroyed by time, age, or careless hands.

I would give you the gift of solitude, the gift of knowing the joy of silence, the chance to be alone and not feel uncomfortable. I would give you transportation for the inner journey and water for your desert places. I want to make you restless with diversion and disenchanted with the artificial excesses of our culture. I would give you a desire to strip life to its essential and the courage to embrace whatever you'll find there.

I would give you sight, the sight that notices the subtleties in nature, in people, and in relationships. I long for you to grasp the meaning of things, to hear the sermons of the seasons, the exhortations of the universe, the warnings of the wounded environment. I would teach you to listen.

I would give you that ability to dance! May you never so tie up your feet with the shackles of responsibility that you can't whirl to the rhythm of the spheres. I would have you embrace the lonely, sweep children into your arms, give wings to the aged, and dance across the barriers of circumstance buoyed by humor and imagination into the ecstasy of joy . . . Yes, I would give you the ability to dance!

I would give you the ability to cry, to feel the pain that shatters the violated, to sense the emptiness of the deserted, to hear the plaintive call of the disoriented and lost, to understand the hopelessness of the powerless. I would give you the sensitivity to cry—for what is locked away, for that which is broken, for those who never knew life, for what was not realized, for the least and the last to know freedom.

I would give you the gift of gratitude. I would have you appreciate the gift of where you've come from and who brought you to where you are. May each day you live be a liturgy of praise you sing at Sun's setting. May you dwell upon the gift of what is, not wasting your energies on what could have been.

I would give you the gift of integrity, that you would be truthful at any cost, bound by your word; that you would make honest judgments, even against yourself at times; that you would be just and have pure motives. I would have you realize that you are accountable first, individually to God alone, and then second, to yourself. I would have you choose right, even if it is not popular or understood, even by those who love you.

I would give you the impulse and ability to pray, knowing that in your relationship with God there is much to be said, and God is the one who must say it. I would have you know the difference between prayer and piety; I would make you aware that prayer often has no words but only an open, vulnerable accessibility to God's love, mercy, grace, and justice. I would hope that you discover that prayer is an awareness of your need, a knowledge without which there is no growth or becoming. I would have you, my child, know through experience and example that there is nothing too insignificant to lay before God, yet in that openness we often find Him lifting us above what we brought to Him. I would have prayer teach you that what we so often think we seek is not on the list of what we need, yet God does not upbraid us for our seeking but delights in our coming to Him, even when we don't understand. Mostly, I would have you know that true prayer is synonymous with gratitude and contentment, and discover the marvelous outlet prayer is for communicating this delight with God.

Lastly, I would teach you to soar, to rise above the common, yet find delight in the commonplace; to fly over the distracting disturbances of life, yet see from this perspective ways to attack the knotty problems that thwart people's growth and stymie their development. I would give wings to your dreams and insight to see beyond the now. I would have those wings develop strength from much use so that others may be born aloft on your wings when life becomes too weighty for them to bear. At last, those wings, I know, will take you high and away from the reach of all of us who have taught you, to places we have together dreamed of. We will watch and cheer as you fade from our view into vistas grand and new, and we will be glad.

Gloria Gaither

BOB DOLE

Bob Dole is one of our nation's foremost political figures. Senator Bob Dole's career of public service has made a difference for America. Dole grew up on the plains of western Kansas. His distinguished career includes Senate majority leader, chairman of the Senate Finance Committee, a candidate for president, his party's nominee for vice president, a member of the House of Representatives, the chairman of the Republican Party, a state legislator, and a county attorney. During World War II, Dole was gravely wounded on the battlefield in 1945, and was twice decorated for heroic achievement. His decorations include two Purple Hearts and a Bronze Star with Oak Leaf Cluster. Senator Dole is married to Elizabeth Hanford Dole, president of the American Red Cross. They reside in Washington, D.C.

Dear Baby,

It's a pleasure to be among the first to welcome you to the world! You are fortunate to have been born at such an exciting time, and in the greatest country on earth.

You will one day realize how special America is—a land of precious freedom and boundless opportunity. As you grow older, I would encourage you to follow your hopes and dreams, to never forget those who sacrificed to make those dreams possible, and to always stand up for what you believe is right.

You will experience many blessings during your life. There will also be times when life won't seem so easy. During tough times, I have been inspired by the motto of my home state of Kansas: "*Ad astra per apsera*—To the stars through difficulties." Perhaps those words will one day be helpful to you too.

Take comfort in the fact that most adults realize our children are our future, and never forget that as long as we continue striving to leave a better nation for the generation that follows, America's best days will always be ahead of us.

All my best wishes to you and your parents.

Sincerely,

Bob Dole

CARL HURLEY

Carl Hurley is a wonderful storyteller. A native of Appalachia, Carl delights his audiences with his reflections on life. His unique comedy style, coupled with a background in public education, has earned him the title of "America's funniest professor."

Dear Baby,

Welcome to your new world. I think you'll find it a very interesting place to live. According to the latest information we have, there's no place like it in the universe.

I must tell you that your stay here will seem very brief, even if you live to a ripe old age. On the brighter side, it can be a wonderful experience if you make it so. Yes, the quality of life you have is to a large extent up to you.

My advice is to build into your life what I call the three Ls. They stand for Love, Learning, and Laughter.

Through your love of others, you will realize great joy. Learn to love and let it grow. It's habit forming.

Learning leads to a richer life and a better understanding of people. That leads to a higher level of caring. The world certainly needs more caring.

Laugh often. Look for the humor in life. You'll soon learn that the world is a funny place. See the humor and share it with others. Laughter helps bring people together and forms the bonds on which lasting friendships are built.

Love and Learning will help you experience life to its fullest. And please don't forget Laughter—it helps make the other two Ls possible.

Have a great life!

Your friend,

Carl

Carl E. Hurley

Neil Lomax

Neil Lomax was one of the most prolific passers in NCAA history during his career at Portland State University. In his ten-year NFL career Neil earned Pro-Bowl honors in 1984 and 1987. Neil and his family remain active in the Portland area raising money and awareness for Fellowship of Christian Athletes and Young Life. He also hosts a weekly radio program.

Dear Baby,

Welcome to this wonderful world that God created. It is a beautiful place with so many fascinating and exciting things to do and see. I just can't wait for you to see for yourself how good life can be and how special you are to this world and to God. That's right! God thinks you're special! I found out about God and His creation many years ago. You can too!

Our world is full of so many different things—some are not so good and pleasing as others, but you will soon find out what is right and wrong, good and evil. I certainly hope that you have a good mommy and daddy like I have, and they can help you whenever you need them, especially Mom. You'll want to be near her a lot for the next couple of years—especially when you're hungry!

As you grow, you'll experience all this awesome planet has to offer—the cool white foam of the ocean to the fresh, clean sparkling streams that come from the snowcapped mountains over a mile high! But stay close to your Father, for He will provide and protect you from all the danger that comes with this world.

Do what I have done. Get to know your Father not just your earthly mommy and daddy but your heavenly Father. He will always be there—even if Mom and Dad can't. This will be hard, but you will learn to trust, to sacrifice, and to obey your Creator. This is what today is all about—to become a child of God, a friend of your Father's.

Go to sleep little child, and dream sweet dreams about your new and beautiful world. And dream of the day you can call God the Father, your friend.

In His love,
Neil Lomax

Frank Schaeffer

Frank is the son of Dr. Francis and Edith Schaeffer. He produces films, writes books, and lectures on a wide range of cultural and social issues. He is one of America's most outspoken defenders of human life. Frank is perhaps best known, however, for his insights on biblical understanding of Christianity and the arts.

Frank Schaeffer
Newburyport Massachusetts

Dear Baby,
I hope that by the time you are old enough to read this you will know that you cannot know anything! Choose passion over calculation, love ahead of career, and mystery ahead of certainty.

You will find out that what we want and what will happen are always two different things. Do not waste your time trying to change this. Reality is more interesting than anything we can cook up anyway! Providence is infinitely more satisfying than all our best-laid plans. The best part of being alive is life itself.

Love,

Frank Schaeffer

CAROL EVERETT

Carol is a perfect example of someone who writes from a unique perspective. Carol is a tender-hearted advocate for children. She is a former operator of an abortion clinic who now works effortlessly to be a voice for women in crisis pregnancies and as a voice for unborn children.

Carol Everett

Dear Baby,

Welcome to this wonderful world! You are a special creation of God! He designed your nose. He knows what your fingernails look like. He even designed your toes, whether stubby or long!

God has a plan for your life. God chose that special mother and father who would meet your unique needs to grow and to love and to laugh!

As you walk in this world, there will be trying times. Please know that God knew that before you were born and He has a plan for you—not good or better, but His best.

In my life, I've seen death, I've seen pain, and I've seen life. I've watched many struggle to find happiness. Some thought wealth could bring that happiness. Some thought drugs would bring that happiness. Even others thought relationships would bring happiness. My dear baby, if you will simply keep your eyes on the God of this universe, the God who designed you, you will never have the pain that many others experience in life. My prayer for you is that you will choose God's best for your life.

You are a special person, made in the image of God. May He bless you and yours with the fullness of life!

For life in Him,

Carol Everett

LIZ CURTIS HIGGS

Liz Curtis Higgs began her career as a radio personality. She became a professional speaker in 1986 and simply refers to herself as, "An Encourager." In 1995 she received the highest award given for speakers, the Council of Peers Award for Excellence. She is a successful author and columnist and her warmth and caring is absolutely contagious.

Liz Curtis Higgs
AN ENCOURAGER ❤❤

Dear Baby,

Do you know that your parents love you more than even their smiles and tears and sighs and baby talk can possibly communicate?

Do you know that you were prayed for, longed for, waited for, hoped for—for minutes, hours, days, weeks, months, years?

Has anyone told you yet who made you? That you were created by God for a unique purpose, a calling that only you can answer?

Have you heard that God Himself came to earth as a baby, too? That's Christmas—you'll love Christmas!

He lived a perfect life, then died for imperfect us. That's Good Friday, the saddest/happiest day ever.

But then He rose from the dead, and He waits in heaven for us to come home. Wow! That's Easter—you'll love Easter too.

Dear Baby, the days ahead are stacked around your cradle, like gifts waiting to be opened. Tear off the wrapping gently. Live each day fully. And make friends with the One who made you—the best gift of all!

Liz Curtis Higgs

Brennan Manning

Brennan is the author of nine books. He speaks and leads retreats in the U.S. and abroad to people of all ages and backgrounds. His books *Ragamuffin Gospel* and *Abba's Child* have been bestsellers and have been particularly well-received in the music community.

Dear Baby,

God danced the day you were born. What a day of joy as He gave you as a gift to Himself. Through your infancy and teenage years He will continue to rejoice over you, because His love is never based on your performance, never conditional by your moods, and will never know any shadow of change.

I would like to share something that changed my life for good. I learned this from a fellow named Ed Farrell in Detroit.

Ed took a two-week summer vacation to Ireland in order to visit his uncle who was about to celebrate his eightieth birthday. On the morning of the great day, Ed and his uncle got up before dawn, dressed in silence, and went for a walk around the shores of Lake Killarnee. Just as dawn was about to break, his uncle turned to face the rising sun. Ed Farrell didn't know what to do as he stood beside his uncle for twenty full minutes, not a word exchanged. Then his eighty-year-old uncle went skipping down the road, his face radiant with joy. Finally Ed said, "Uncle Seamos, you look very happy. Do you want to tell me why?" His uncle lowered his eyes, tears streaming down his cheeks, and said softly, "The Father is very fond of me. O, me, Father is so very fond of me."

Baby, when someone asks you, "Do you believe God loves you?" You can reply, "He not only loves me, He likes me. In fact, He is very fond of me." There is a wonderful biblical word for Father. It is Abba, which means Daddy. God is your Daddy!

Lovely little one, when your morning and night prayers end with the words, "Abba, I belong to you," your heavenly Father will dance once more.

Under The Mercy

Brennan Manning

Brennan Manning

JOHN FISCHER

John is important not just as a pioneer in what is now considered contemporary Christian music, but for his continued influence as a gifted writer, performer, and teacher. His commentaries on our music, our times, and our culture are insightful and profound. John is a great thinker and has chosen a unique form of expression for his letter.

John Fischer

Dear Baby,

My prayer for you:

I pray that you will one day discover a truly remarkable thing. (It will turn out to be the most important thing you will ever know.) I pray that you will discover that God (yes, the big, wild, unimaginable God who made you, made your parents, made the animals and the earth and the planets and the stars in the heavens), that same God, was once a little baby just like you.

(Hard to believe, isn't it?) But He became a little baby like you so he could grow up and make a way for you and me to know Him and to some day go to heaven and live with Him forever.

That means that even if you and I never meet in this life, we can meet each other in heaven, where we will spend a long time thanking God for what He did to get us there. (You'll find out all about that later. Some of it is kind of sad, but don't worry, because everything's okay now.) So if I don't ever meet you here, that's okay. Just make sure you find me in heaven. Then we can have fun remembering the letter I wrote you before you were even born. And you can tell me all about exactly how you came to find out how very much God loves you.

Yours truly,

John Fischer

Howard G. Hendricks

Howard G. Hendricks is a distinguished professor and chairman of Christian Leadership at Dallas Theological Seminary. He serves on the boards of Walk Through the Bible, Promise Keepers, The Navigators, and Multnomah Bible College. Howard Hendricks is an accomplished author and teacher whose articles often appear in *Decision*, *Moody*, and in *Christianity Today*.

Dear Little One,

   You have been born into our beautiful world that God made, and I'm glad you're here. God created each one of us exactly the way we are, and He sent us to our families at the right time. I hope you will love yours very much. But even more, I pray that you will learn to love God. Then you will help many other people to live better.

   These words are coming to you from an old man. Oh, I don't feel old, but I have lived nearly three-quarters of a century. I have welcomed four children of my own into the world, and also six grandchildren. But above everything else, loving and serving God makes life worthwhile.

   In all of my years, there is nothing more important that I have learned. You see, my mother and father did not know God, and they fought with each other and did not live together. I was a very sad little boy until I heard that Jesus loved me. Then my life changed and I began to live to please Him. After all this time, it just keeps getting better, and I can't wait to go to heaven and meet Him in person. I hope some day you will be there with us too.

   From a friend who wishes you a wonderful life,
   Howard G. Hendricks

DAN QUAYLE

Dan Quayle was born in Indianapolis, Indiana, in 1947. He was elected to Congress at age twenty-nine. He was elected to the Senate at age thirty-three. And Dan Quayle was the Vice President of the United States at the age of forty-one. He continues to be a voice for values of faith, limited government, personal responsibility, and family values.

DAN QUAYLE

Dear Baby:

Having just learned of your arrival, I am proud to welcome you. I also congratulate your mother and father. Whatever else happens in their lives, nothing will ever quite match the joy they are feeling today.

You are entering a very exciting and stimulating world, in which you will find opportunities and experiences that earlier generations could scarcely dream of. Everyone's life is a journey with an unforeseeable path, and my prayer for you is that the journey will bring abundant happiness and contentment. In everything you do, always keep in mind the bedrock principles of faith in God, love of family, and loyalty to the great nation that we are so blessed to call home. All of us are called upon to make thousands of choices in life; adhering to these principles will help you to choose wisely.

The entire Quayle family joins me in extending a warm welcome. Our good wishes go with you all the days of your life. Good luck, and God bless!

Your Special Letter

This letter was written especially for you by:

_____

_____

_____

_____

_____

_____

_____

_____

Dear Baby,

_____

_____

_____

_____

_____

_____

_____

_____

_____

_____

_____

_____

_____

_____

_____

_____